Reflection
and Other Plays

T0345252

NEW INDIAN PLAYWRIGHTS

MAHESH ELKUNCHWAR

Reflection
and Other Plays

LONDON NEW YORK CALCUTTA

Seagull Books, 2018

Original plays © Mahesh Elkunchwar
Translation and introductory material © Seagull Books, 2018
This compilation © Seagull Books, 2018

ISBN 978 0 8574 2 494 5

British Library Cataloguing-in-Publication Data
A catalogue record for this book is available from the British Library

Typeset by Manasij Dutta, Seagull Books, Calcutta, India
Printed and bound by Hyam Enterprises, Calcutta, India

CONTENTS

THERE IS NO HOMECOMING

Mahesh Elkunchwar in Conversation with Anuradha Kapur

This long conversation with Mahesh Elkunchwar took place over three days and it was a time for slow thinking and listening, habits I see diminishing fast. The conversation meandered and zigzagged. Such zizags, or sideways moves, are precious for they break an oppositional line; they hope to find instead what Svetlana Boym calls 'alternative archaeology' for practices (2017: 118).

Mahesh's corpus of work is large and varied. He has been writing since the 1960s. His plays and, of late, his essays, have tackled thoughts on identity, suppressed and expressed violence, orthodoxy and heterodoxy, urbanization and the city. He writes up a nuanced set of responses to industrial and urban society—the city as a place of contradiction, fantasy and dream, of anonymity and freedom, of inexplicable alienation as well as sudden camaraderie. In some senses, he appears to work with the complexity of modernism itself, as a form made possible by fragmentation and movement—dislocated spaces and migration. Mahesh has also written columns in newspapers and taught English for years at Nagpur University.

Through our conversation, we hoped that a sort of lateral connection could be made between Mahesh's corpus of work and his person—a reconsideration of the words *person* (one whose life is biographically accounted for or narrativized), *persona* (one who has a literary and cultural role) and a *personage* (one who is an important or influential figure). After all, a playwright creates characters but is also created by the *category* 'playwright' (see Boym 1991 for an elaboration of this idea). In marking a zigzag path through all the inflections of *persona*, derived from Latin and meaning mask or character played by an actor, am I saying that the person and persona of Mahesh are unambiguously linked? That Mahesh always writes an 'autobiography', the story of his life, over again? Or repeatedly stages his own literary fictions upon himself?

I am hoping to work more with chiaroscuro to capture the conversations, and to explore who it is who stands in the wings and who it is who enters the stage and takes up what role and at what time.

I hope that this will be a playful exercise in the near and the far, much as writing for the theatre is an activity that works with the microscope and the telescope.

ANURADHA KAPUR. Do you work with nostalgia? Svetlana Boym describes nostalgia as '[T]he relationship between individual biography and the biography of groups or nations, between personal and collective memory, individual home and collective homeland' (2002: 14) I ask because you write a great deal about the past—the Wada Trilogy, for example—sounds your own past as well.

MAHESH ELKUNCHWAR. I don't think I work with nostalgia. My childhood was not enjoyable. Just as the reference to the past is not always happy, I have no longing to return to a time and space pendant in the past. But I do go back to my past to analyse, to reassess my early years in a detached manner, hoping to understand myself as I am today.

My mother came to our house nearly a hundred years ago. The house was more than a hundred years old, built sometime in 1875. The women in the wada, the home, were flagbearers of tradition. They moulded lives in ways that were almost invisible but entirely material. The wada, however, changed continuously. Nothing remains the same. As I said: Changes are constant, some apparent and some not. While nothing remains the same, something does as well, something vital actually remains—as we well know. To that extent, there is something eternal about a changing, adapting, modifying journey.

So. Time is continuous. As a writer, I do not fragment time. But even if it is continuous, it is not linear. And it helps me understand myself in the present. I analyse situations and characters and therefore also myself, through different points of views, facets, features and aspects. Mindsets and contrasting responses shape my work. As also *produce me* and my viewing glass.

I had a comfortable distance from the wada because I grew up with my uncle who was a lawyer in Yavatmal. My brother was a trained vocalist who could never fulfil his ambition to be a singer and spent most of his life in the Wada. Zamindars' children were not supposed to perform. He was not a rebel but he never forgave himself, nor our father, nor the entire feudal system that did not allow him to do what was most vital for him. It was not only women who suffered. Men did too.

In 1967, my nieces and nephews (my brother's children) came to live with me in Nagpur. My sister-in-law was a wise woman, a great reader and much ahead of her times. She felt her children had to be urbanized. Land laws had changed in late 1949 because of which we had lost a large part of our lands. She understood that only urbanization would help the children get away from the stifling orthodoxies of the wada. She did not want her children to duplicate the lives of the women of the wada, who lived and died in that one space while life changed and transformed around them. The tenacity of Indian women amazes me—how they rise above difficult circumstance and achieve dignity. My mother loved reading; she had a teacher who would come home to teach English conversation. That was before she came into the Elkunchwar household. Then everything changed for her.

My father died in 1975. My mother came to stay with me in 1978. It was when I was 40 that another kind of time was spent, by my mother and me, in my home. Being away from home all my life, I hardly knew my mother. The routine was different from the one lived out in the wada, the rhythm and tempo were different. A new set of adult relationships were being forged. It's difficult to give a name to that relationship but it was a kind of friendship.

ANURADHA KAPUR. The resonance with the Wada Trilogy is profound and deep in the way you articulate your own journey. A certain verticality comes to mind in the way you excavate the Wada and its memories.

MAHESH ELKUNCHWAR. I was at an advantage when I wrote *Wada Chirebandi*: I was away from it most of the time and yet I was an integral part of it. I visited it often, but more like a visitor and that helped me with a sort of distancing. What interested me as a writer was to see how people cope with constant change. Human beings were at the centre. Fortunately, my father, my mother and my siter-in-law were all wise people and it was at their insistence that all of us left home very early in our lives, that we were given a decent education and that we never had to see the plight of the Deshpandes in the trilogy.

But I was also surrounded by people who were not so wise and who surrendered themselves to decline. When I wrote the play, I knew I was not going to highlight the political or social aspect of that life. Rather, I wanted to write about characters trapped in an irrevocable situation. Political or social situations are mostly topical. And if a writer cannot go beyond the topicality, he ends up writing inferior work.

That is why the political aspect of a life, when it appears as an undercurrent, is far more telling. Undercurrents can be of all kinds and can flow in different directions simultaneously. Undercurrents toss and turn human beings and thence form them. We are flung about and shaped.

I am not interested in mapping political movements either, except in the way in which they may appear as an underlying utterance, as implicit meaning, as a current below the surface.

ANURADHA KAPUR. So would you say that, in your work, time is *both* vertical and horizontal? And that, therefore, you don't work with nostalgia. In your [Wada] trilogy, therefore, you do not obliterate history with the objective of returning to the time of your childhood or youth. The slower, more humane rhythms of a time gone by do not enthral you nor hold you captive—you don't travel back into space because you're homesick. At the same time, you do not accept the idea that time gone by is time gone by—vanished without residue. Rather, you seem to say that there is always residue, and that it helps fashion something for the future. So you hold up this looking backwards as a device that helps refract your ideas of home, belongingness and change in the present.

Going with Boym, nostalgia can also be a critical device to examine the unrealized dreams of the past so they might channel into the needs and dreams of the future. A device to view the near and the far, to feel both engaged and estranged at the same time (see Boym 2002).

So, if there is no homecoming, what is your relationship to space?

MAHESH ELKUNCHWAR. There is no homecoming. Once it is lost, it is lost. But that is when one creates. It is a reason, an incentive and finally a reward for what you have lost.

Eugene O'Neill said that life is sickness. I did not agree with him, although I could perceive his suffering. Why do people suffer? I began to isolate situations, people trapped in such situations, and tried to understand the suffering. Is there no way out of it? That made me turn to the Saddarsana, the six major schools of Indian philosophy. My grooming in Sanskrit helped me there.

So I read philosophy and struggled with the spiritual as I attempted to transcend what was around me, my material time and space. Reading philosophy and learning spiritual texts were the two tools that I had at my disposal to help me make an escape from a space that was inhibiting and time that appeared restrictive.

In both art and philosophical practice, time and space have a territory without a horizon. Once the horizons disappear, therefore, both become meaningless concepts. It is at this place, this indistinguishable space, where everything happens. That is where *life* happens. That is the point of supreme reality and all art aspires to get there.

As a mortal human being, I am bound by, and to, time and space. Nevertheless, I try to transcend them. So that I may to move to a place that is infinite. It is not easy for a writer, almost impossible. But a Kishori Amonkar can do so. Kumar Gandharva also comes to mind. When they sing, they are in a territory beyond the grasp of the intellect. Unlike my 'spirituality' which is entirely intuitional.

Music awakens a dreamworld within you, a world not accessible to our intellect. It is indefinable, unnameable, indescribable, unspecifiable. As a writer, I use words, words created by human intelligence. Words cannot describe, or we cannot produce words, to describe the indescribable. The word is overused material. The word can propose a philosophical treatise—but a *sur* [melody] can transport us to this unspecifiable territory of experience. Words can move one but not necessarily exalt one. The word is not a pure tool the way in which a *sur* is. The word is artificial, created by human intellect. So how can it transcend the limits of that very intellect? The *sur*, on the other hand, is natural and has a pristine purity. Unburdened by any associations, it is pure material. I think it is Susan Langar who said that all arts try to be music. So right.

I think all artists struggle to free themselves from the constraints of time and space, to go beyond time and space, into the timeless and spaceless. Funnily enough, they have to use these same tools to go beyond them.

So, with my limited resources and the inadequacy of the tools at my disposal, I embarked on a journey, hoping to achieve at least a little of what music does. Once I realized that, I stopped being illustrative, expansive. I stopped using so many words. Because, doing that, I was watering down my experience. I decided to not even try to say that which is unsayable, but, rather, to keep it in deliberately created loaded silences. The dialogue created around these silences was a mere a pointer to those silences, and were meant to evoke the right responses in actors and audience alike.

That is why I expect my actors need to have a complex understanding in order to flesh out that which is unsaid. The real play is in the subtext, and the actor has to ferret that out. Unfortunately, they prefer to stay on the surface, thinking *that* is the play.

This naturally makes one think of life. One tries to understand life in its totality—which is an almost impossible task unless you are a seer. To be aware of a reality which produces our mundane reality is not so easy. One may not understand it in totality, but one can choose a moment and try to probe it. Because every moment is a condensed eternity.

I am fully aware of my mortality. The materiality of my existence is never ruled out in my mind. The question to ask is: Am I equally aware of my mind? Full of contradiction, of pain, of guilt?

I see the contradiction between body and mind as the tool with which to attempt an understanding of myself.

ANURADHA KAPUR. Actors are very interested in this duality, and come face to face with it at every rehearsal. How do they materialize thought? Through action. In the actor's vocabulary, *action* is *thought* or *thought* is *action*. In that sense, an actor's body, or all bodies for that matter, have no secure boundaries demarcating the psychological from the social, or the biological from the ideological, that is to say, the abstract from the material, the material from the immaterial. Actors transmit emotion, and it is caught by the spectators as a sort of contagion (see Fischer-Lichte 2005 and 2008 for a complex discussion of this metaphor). It is transformative when experienced by both actor and spectator.

For me, the jewellery sequence in *Virasat* comes to mind or, again from *Virasat*, the image of the grandmother. Enclosed and cocooned in her own world. Her senses still awake but her compass is askew and her clock is barely moving. That still figure transmits an ineffable sense to us, tells us that, while she is crumbling away, she is steadfastly present. Particles of time and space group around her.

MAHESH ELKUNCHWAR. If a writer has the quality of *vishva-vatslya* or compassion, then s/he is a great writer. Dostoyevsky wrote about gamblers and losers, but with such understanding and love. Like a mother who loves the most her challenged child. All good writers aspire to do that.

ANURADHA KAPUR. And failures. There is in your work a recurring theme of people falling prey—in *Vaasana Kand,* in *Sultan*, in *Holi*—to lynching, blindness, viciousness. You fashion these people and put them before your spectators. In *Holi*, for example, by visibilizing the unaccountable viciousness that overtakes a group of students, you bring the perpetrators into view, into consideration. Into being counted, *now* within the present. And thereby you engage with questions of dignity as they are understood both outside and inside the theatrical frame. Putting them out there, denuded as it were, is a different strategy from divesting the middle class of its hypocrisies. It is, instead, a reflection on dignity by way of indignity. Sometimes to understand the profound meaning of dignity, we must show indignity on stage.

MAHESH ELKUNCHWAR. My heart has always gone out to the marginalized. One has seen how an individual can be hunted down and destroyed by a frenzied mob, stripping him of what is most precious to any human being—his dignity.

I do not know how mobs come into being. Is it always the insecure, the mediocre non-entities that want to belong and come together and that have a sense of power by herding together and getting drunk on it? How is a mob made? Do we have to be a herd? The urge to make a decision is replaced with something else, a herd mentality.

I was 27 when I wrote *Holi*. About a herd, a mob, ready to destroy a life that they thought was against their lifestyle. They are talking about Hindutva* these days, 'our lifestyle, our culture', ruling out any other lifestyle and culture. Real Hinduism, as I understand it, has always been all-encompassing, all-embracing, plural, welcoming all noble thoughts no matter where they come from. *Aa no bhadrah kratwo yantu wishwatah*—this is a Vedic mantra—Let noble thoughts come to me from all directions (Rig Veda 1.89.1). That is the basic precept of Hinduism. It proposes a place for everybody, respect for everybody, love and understanding for everybody. The beauty of Hinduism is it that asks you, first, in no uncertain terms to acknowledge your share of guilt rather than to assign blame. It shows you the ways to self-purification.

Parag does exactly that in the third part of the trilogy. There is redemption, if you face yourself squarely, honestly, with humility. Hinduism does not dangle a carrot of hope in front of you, but it gives you the courage to tread a path of self-purification. A walk on a razor's edge. There is nothing romantic about Hinduism. It is stark, brutally down to earth. My intuitive motto is: Acceptance of life. As it comes. Never allowing myself to forget my share in the moulding of it. I try to think of this in a non-hierarchical way, a plane rather than a pyramid.

ANURADHA KAPUR. In the ritual of shraadha,† the ant too has a place.

---

* A right-wing nationalist ideology seeking to establish the hegemony of upper-caste Hindus and the Hindu way of life. It is the official ideology of the ruling Bharatiya Janata Party (BJP).

† A Hindu ritual performed for one's ancestors, especially deceased parents.

Inside the frame of theatre, dignity is often restored or reinvented by several different kinds of grammars: that of reflexivity where the co-presence of actors and spectators might produce *reflections* on indignity, so that we might think together about systems of social injustice. But also through affect, and feeling—through these too we might reflect on dignity. By pointing to the unspeakable calamities that befall un-accommodated man, we feel the human condition. As we take cover from the calamities that befall us, we recognize *each other* as humans.

MAHESH ELKUNCHWAR. My grandmother had a great affection for a mentally challenged young man in my village. Not pity but compassion and real love. Maybe this notion and need to accept has come to me from my grandmother. To understand the compulsions of others, for we are the manifestations of the same life. But, and this is important, even when we are the same, one life is not the same as another. And this fascinates me. Every unit is a complete unit and worthy of respect.

I was a compulsive reader as a child. Produced a sensible, (as being *sensed*, as being *cognizable*) reality in my mind and even composed dialogues. Muttered these dialogues to myself and created an illusory world. These were means to be connected. A connect in reality was denied to me, so I created it in an illusory world. Which also means that I was lonely.

But even as I made up stories—perhaps subconsciously training myself to create characters, situations, dialogue, a sort of preparation for a future playwright—I was interested in experience and not plot. Experience is not plot.

ANURADHA KAPUR. Though you're excellent at structuring plots.

MAHESH ELKUNCHWAR. I am not interested in argument, denouement or finale. Is there any such thing as 'Final'? Like in Indian music, I want to expand one mode. I begin with an experience, and attempt to expand that. So I set out to flesh out an experience. Structuring it is a matter of craft. One learns it by trial and error.

Pratibimb (*Reflection*) came to me in a flash. I was looking at the jacket picture of Hebert Marcuse's *One-Dimensional Man*. A man looking into the mirror sees only his back. I thought: Supposing we do not have a reflection at all? It was an unsettling thought. Why do we want to be reassured all the time of our existence?

It was around this time that I branched out into writing essays. They gave me a great freedom to delve deep within. Theatre, in any case, had sort of disillusioned me. They say it is a collective art and all that. In my innocence, I thought we shall enrich ourselves together. In practise, I discovered that everyone connected with theatre had his/her own agenda and that the agenda was more important than any probe or quest. I stopped writing plays for eight years. And arrived at the essay. Writing plays is like playing cricket—you are part of a team. But writing essays is like swimming—you are alone with your water, there is nobody to make demands on you. Freedom.

The essays began in 1981. They are really belles-lettres, literary pieces. Uncategorized: autobiography, memoir, creative composition? My essay-writing has not been very prolific. I begin with an instance from my life and then branch out in many directions—philosophy, psychology, anthropology, literature, music. I enjoy it. I also enjoyed writing a column in the newspaper where I introduced classic modernist texts, like Sartre's writing. But that was a secondary activity.

I'm more relaxed when I write an essay. I believe an essay is like a soliloquy—it's about a private, emotional life. But it should not remain private or personal. I want to remove the 'I'-ness of the piece. It has to rise above the 'I'-ness and become a universal experience.

You know what? Youngsters have started dramatizing my essays. Because I do not have any new play to show. In a way, it is gratifying to know that they see dramatic possibilities in my essays too.

ANURADHA KAPUR. Raymond Williams marks three kinds of conventions, among others, in composing a play—dialogue, monologue and soliloquy (1985: 32–64). Dialogue can mark different positions and exchanges between people, spoken by named characters and arranged as alternating conversation; a monologue is delivered by persons who speak *by* themselves in the presence of others or alone. The monologue might also suggest the sort of speech energy that overwhelms or monopolizes other conversation. And soliloquy is a form of speech where the character talks *to* herself or himself. A philosophical debate with yourself—between a divided self, between yourself and your different faculties. It is about the *process* of thinking and you may or may not find a conclusion, a solution or an outcome (ibid.: 31–64)

I think you use all three in your plays, these different modes of address. Particularly in Wada Trilogy, and *Sonata*, where all three intertwine. You write up a different mode for each play as well, like the three plays of the trilogy. The long reflections of Parag, Chandu and Abhay on life and dignity and freedom, are soliloquies. But they are also essays, also tracts. And the actor needs to find an appropriate mode—of speech, voice and body—to render these.

Then there is the essay-soliloquy, as it were, an essay which is also a soliloquy, and a soliloquy which is composed as an essay. This, a mix of formal conventions, is as readable as it is performable.

I find these different planes of writing interesting as textual work but also as acting work, where the performer must form and reform under the audience's gaze to enunciate these words.

To be honest, I don't believe that there is any 'willing suspension of disbelief' in theatre as practice. In your plays, certainly, there is no suspension of disbelief in order to enter your plot frame. You lay out a series of what I suggest are *contracts* for the audience to agree upon, and thereafter it 'plays' according to the rules of the game that you have drawn up for it in your writing. This is most sharply visible in the Wada Trilogy, in *Sonata*, in *Holi,* in *Atmakatha (Autobiography)*, as well as in your essays.

In any case, a genre is not water tight, is it? It is not some ideal type with a rigid set of rules. It can be made practicable through different combinations and permutations so as to *style* social processes in particular formal ways.

MAHESH ELKUNCHWAR. All you have said is absolutely true. I lay down my conditions and those who are prepared to surrender to them may enjoy my work. People who are hopelessly conditioned about what constitutes real theatre may be disappointed by me. They are, in fact. Writing was never a top priority for me. That is why I never understood the compulsion of making theatre a career.

The word career itself is something I resist, I suppose. I didn't make a career out of my teaching or my writing. In the 1970s, Vijaya Mehta suggested that I go to Mumbai because it would be better for my career. And I thought: Do I want to be a professional writer? Career means material success. Particularly money. A different kind of focus and efficiency.

Teaching, on the other hand, was a vocation. I did not accept the principalship of a college because teaching for me was not about rising to a higher or senior position. Teaching gave me a connect. It was not self-gratification or a desire to reproduce. It was an effort at producing awareness.

In time I realized that neither writing nor teaching were my top priority. My top priority was living. And my theatre is a by-product of that. I like to remind myself that children play for hours, completely engrossed, lost even. They do not stop even when it is dark, and have to be dragged back home for homework. It is just like that for me. I enjoy living so much that, unless driven by an inner compulsion, I do not write. It's important to go out and play. You can't be tasked to write—that is what I believe. I didn't churn out anything for eight years between 1973 to 1983. I had nothing to lose. There was nothing at stake. I hadn't built such a reputation that I needed to protect it.

I stumbled into theatre. I saw a Tendulkar play,* directed by Vijaya-bai†
and that evening changed my life. I thought: This is something I can do, this
is something I have been wanting to do. Tendulkar and Vijaya-bai were both
catalysts. Had I only *read* Tendulkar, I mightn't have turned to writing. It was
the magic of the performance.

I wrote a series of one-act plays after that and they were published in
Satykatha, the most prestigious magazine of the time. (It is extinct now.) And
one fine morning I got a letter from Vijay-bai, saying she wanted to direct those
plays. There was no looking back after that.

Even then, I never became an industrious writer. I wrote sporadically, only
when I wanted to. That is why Mumbai and its glitter did not attract me. Somehow, wealth and fame have never impressed me. But learning has. Does. Always.

Then I got the coveted Homi Bhabha Fellowship, with no strings attached.
I travelled extensively all over India and Europe, met a lot of people. All that
was quite enriching. But then I returned to my cocoon. I didn't have to be a
part of that glittering world for my personal growth.

I've never bothered to find out if I've contributed anything to Theatre. But
I have consistently analysed whether I have grown because of my theatre. How
can *I contribute?*—it is so presumptuous. No artist is bigger than his medium.

There was dissatisfaction with the theatre at one point. I had a deep connect with Vijaya and shared an energetic, artistic dialogue. In 1971, Vijaya
moved into professional theatre. The place, time and space for dialogue
changed thereafter. Different pressures, different theatre economies. We
remained friends. That was when *Garbo, Vaasnakand* and *Party* were written.
Sometimes I felt that a similar connect with other directors was missing. I felt

---

* Vijay Tendulkar (1928–2008): renowned Marathi playwright, movie and television
writer, literary essayist, political journalist and social commentator.

† Vijaya Mehta (b. 1934): film and theatre director and actor. Co-founder of Mumbai-
based theatre group Rangayan. She is best known for her role in *Party* (1984). A leading
figure in the experimental Marathi theatre of the 1960s.

that theatre was not a collective activity any more. That it was pulling in different directions, each to their own. For me, no make-up, no sets, no large cast, no large numbers. Municipal-school halls were good—barebones venues that made the work immediate and accessible. And that for me was what undergirded the theatre practice and its collectivities. If this was not attainable, I thought, then I should stop writing.

Surrounded by friends and family, I was happy and fulfilled. I began learning Indian texts, the Saddarsana to be precise, from an erudite scholar. For five years, he taught me the major texts. It was a glorious time, and a most profound experience of learning.

Perhaps this was one reason for the joy of theatre paling for a time. When My guruji died, it was a great loss. My mother fell ill. I spent time at the wada. I spent time with my brother and sister-in-law. It was then that I had the idea of writing on the wada, in the wada. The first draft was done within a week. With *Wada* began my second phase of writing. When I understood that I should write only when I am ready.

ANURADHA KAPUR. What is at stake if you fail?

MAHESH ELKUNCHWAR. Nothing! An inner connect was a desperate need, though. Theatre and teaching provided that. Teaching did not disappoint. It was a substitute for the theatre and vice versa.

ANURADHA KAPUR. Is teaching reproducing?

MAHESH ELKUNCHWAR. For me it was not. It was a friendship. A creative occupation. A connect without pain, perhaps. Was it sublimation? Balm? Substitution? We need to analyse dispassionately what friendship is.

ANURADHA KAPUR. Boym says friendship is an 'elective affinity without finality, a relationship without plot or place in our society, an experience for its own sake. It is not always democratic or egalitarian, but rather selective and not entirely inclusive' (2009–10).

I see several planes of friendship in your plays, arranged differently on each plane. Let me extrapolate a bit here, keeping in mind some of the friendships you delineate in your texts.

Friendships are webs of reciprocities and complementarities that come about because we elect our friends; because with them we find some sort of rapport, kinship, resonance. Apart from the Wada Trilogy, I am thinking of the complex trails secreted by the characters in *Sonata*. And a web gets woven by these trails as a web is spun by the spider. The spider's web is not outside the spider—it is generated *in* and *by* the spider itself. Just as making anything is generated in the artist herself, *in* her body, *in* her memory and *in* the act— and that is part of the *action* of making. Tim Ingold citing John Berger says, 'You become what you draw' (2013: 128)

In *Holi*, entirely combustible relationships come into view but also those that are fireproof, non-flammable and lasting, and these appear by staging the very opposite of friendship—extreme and senseless provocation and violence.

Friendships question hierarchy. Even as they shine a powerful beam of light on people, they work just as well with shadow. I think of Abhay and Parag. I think of *Sonata* again. I think of Nandini and Parag. Friendship provides an etiquette of living, a code of conduct, a grammar for functioning in life. So it is even a sort of practice (Boym 2009–10). Parag and Nadini devise a code of conduct in a perplexing world. And live by it. So friendships finds unlikely ways of resolving problems that are as old as the hills: How to live together in a world of immeasurable differences and bewildering uncertainty. How to overcome the blocks that such differences immediately massify into.

MAHESH ELKUNCHWAR. Friendship—total trust. Where one can lay bare one's vulnerabilities without fear of being judged.. Acceptance of another being in undemanding deep love. Respect for him/her. No material expectations. No birthdays.This, of course, must not be, cannot be confused with romantic love. Friendship grows but love can die. Friendship is lasting, solid, a commitment without being a burden. It is the greatest joy to see a friendship blossoming into maturity.

Although I come from a small village, I think it has given me a certain edge over many urban writers. That does not mean that I write about rural themes. Not at all. But I have experienced a deep connect among village folks (gone now) which I missed in the urban life I was living. That is reflected in *Wada* (I hope). I am a completely urbanized person now—my job, my reading, my travels, my friends, my theatre, all these have made me what I am today. Yet I am forever looking for the deep connect in all this, a connect similar to the one I experienced in my childhood.

My family is also greatly responsible for this urban spirit. My father, my mother, although they spent their lives in a village, had an active contact with the outside urban world, mainly through reading and travelling. Our wada has a 15-foot-high fortification wall. It insulated us in a way. I do not know if it was good or bad.

When I started writing in 1967, Tendulkar was in his prime. I liked his work but I knew I did not want to write like him. My concerns, my preoccupations, my compulsions were so totally different. People say that the modernity in my work is because of Tendulkar. That is only partially true. The fact is, the 60s were a time of radical changes in Marathi literature, radical changes overflowing from 1950, from Mardhekar.* From 1950 onwards, new poetry, new short stories, new novels, they all changed the face of staid Marathi literature. The entire literary climate was pervaded with a spirit of newness, experimentation. That atmosphere spilt over to our theatre. Tendulkar is a product of that atmosphere, let us not forget. I had the added advantage of sowing my seeds in a soil already prepared by him.

And what is modernity? Writing about topical issues? Holding a flag? Making strident noises about 'the enemy'?

Fundamentals never change. Writers have been throwing light on different aspects of it from time immemorial. If I succeed in throwing light on one of its

---

* B. S. Mardhekar (1909–56): A writer who brought about a radical shift of sensibility in Marathi poetry and, influenced by modernists, introduced a decadent urban ethos in it.

aspects, hitherto unknown—then I am modern. We all use the same torch. What we light and how, that's what decides if we are modern. And the modern is not necessarily good just by virtue of it being modern.

ANURADHA KAPUR. The torch you talk of reveals darknesses as well: shadows and crannies, darkened tracks and fault lines.

I want to reflect on the delicate connections you make between the country and the city, between the feudal, the urban and the cosmopolitan, especially in the Wada Trilogy.

Raymond Williams reminds us that country means both land and nation. It can mean an entire societal structure, and it can mean landmass. Similarly, *desh* [homeland], *pradesh* [region], *rashtra* [state] and *samaj* [society] are interrelated words and invoke powerful feelings. Around the word rural (land), many ideas have gathered—of serenity, innocence, virtue and goodness. But also of backwardness, ignorance, limitation. Around the city has gathered the idea of an 'achieved centre'—of learning, communication and brightness but also hostile associations of dissonance, worldliness, ambition and decadence. The rural settlement has been of different kinds, and its organization

> has varied from the tribe and the manor to the feudal estate, from the small peasantry and tenant farmers to the rural commune, from the *latifundia* and the plantation to the large capitalist enterprise and the state farm. The city, no less, has been of many kinds: state capital, administrative base, religious centre, market-town, port and mercantile depot, military barracks, industrial concentration (Williams 1973: 1–2).

Your characters inhabit many of these spaces and journey across them. During those journeys, those crossings, faultlines appear—of paths taken and abandoned, or abandoned and forgotten, or taken and realized. Some characters remain on track, some go *off track*. I think particularly of Chandu and Abhay, Sudhir and Anjali, as also of Ranju and Parag. They ask us to reconsider our understanding of being, as it were, off track.

To their various tracks, I add a word: *cosmopolitan.*

The word cosmopolitan comes from the Greek, meaning 'citizen of the world'. It suggests that all humans are to be regarded as citizens of a universal *state* of humankind and that they have moral duties to one another beyond their immediate and particular domains of race, gender, ethnicity, nationality, religion. Our obligations to one another are founded on our humanity alone. This is what obliges us to treat a stranger with grace and hospitality if she happens to come into our territory (see Felluga 2015 for a short and clear annotation of the word cosmopolitan).

But then: Chandu, cosmopolitan? Abhay, cosmopolitan by the same measure as Chandu? Does the word have such a large un-graduated sweep?

I want to invoke the cosmopolitan *principle* here with reference to Abhay and Chandu as well.

Travelling and journeying and being a stranger is integral to the cosmopolitan principle. Travelling defamiliarizes our routine, everyday world. It expands the idea we have of our reality. By encountering different people and places, we incorporate them into our imaginations and so effect a sort of transformation. The experience of multiple identifications changes who we are and how we see the world. It may even cause us to see that one's society may in some ways require the presence of the stranger so that we see our own selves from another perspective.

The journeying of Abhay and Chandu, both in radically different spaces and climes is about *processing* lives. They learn as they go along: they learn about being alone but not forsaken, about struggling to communicate in hostile spaces, and about being understood and, equally often, misunderstood. They learn about hospitality and generosity and sometimes the opposite of that as well. Their travels are *them* in a sense—their journeying trails are that which makes them human.

In the Trilogy particularly, the call for ethical relationships with one another, and the tracking of these relationships through various zones of time and place—feudal, rural, urban and, poignantly, the cosmopolitan—creates an intricate pattern. Sometimes that is illumined in your texts, and at other times seen as shadow play.

READINGS

BOYM, Svetlana. 1991. *Death in Quotation Marks: Cultural Myths of the Modern Poet*. Cambridge, MA: Harvard University Press.

———. 2002. *The Future of Nostalgia*. New York: Basic Books.

———. 2009–10. 'Scenography of Friendship'. *Cabinet* 36 (Winter). Available at: http://cabinetmagazine.org/issues/36/boym.php (last accessed on 9 January 2018).

———. 2017. *The Off Modern*. London and New York: Bloomsbury.

FELLUGA, Dino Franco. 2015. *Critical Theory: The Key Concepts*. London and New York: Routledge.

FISCHER-LICHTE, Erika. 2005. *Theatre, Sacrifice, Ritual: Exploring Forms of Political Theatre*. London and New York: Routledge.

———. 2008. *The Transformative Power of Performance: A New Aesthetics* (Saskya Iris Jain trans.). London and New York: Routledge.

INGOLD, Tim. 2013. *Making: Anthropology, Archaeology, Art and Architecture*. London and New York: Routledge.

WILLIAMS, Raymond. 1973. *The Country and the City*. London: Chatto & Windus.

———. 1985. *Writing in Society*. London: Verso.

FLOWER OF BLOOD

(Raktapushp)

TRANSLATED BY SHANTA GOKHALE

Flower of Blood was first performed in Hindi as a Theatre Unit Production at Prithvi Theatre Workshop, Bombay, on 5 February 1981. It was later performed in Marathi, with the same director and almost the same cast. The credits given below are of the Hindi production.

BHAU	Amareesh Puri
PADMA	Suneela Pradhan
LILU	Varsha Kothari
RAJA	Suneel Shanbag
DIRECTION	Satyadev Dubey
PRODUCTION IN-CHARGE	Hemant Rege
LIGHTING	Premnath Sav
SOUND	Nishant Suri, Hareesh Patel

One half of the stage is the sitting room. The other half is Raja's room. A foot-high platform at the back of the sitting room leads to Padma's room. There are two doors to the sitting room—one for going out, the other into the house. It is five o'clock in the evening. Bhau and Padma are in the sitting room.

BHAU. So how did you spend your day?

PADMA. Doing nothing.

BHAU. Why?

PADMA. No reason.

BHAU. How's the cardigan coming along?

PADMA. It's coming along.

BHAU. Where? It can't come along if you just sit there with the wool and needles in your hands.

PADMA. I'm fed up with it.

BHAU. Winter is nearly here.

PADMA. So?

BHAU. It doesn't look as if we'll be able to go out this year.

PADMA. Makes no difference.

BHAU. Why are you so cynical? We might go. Where's Leeli?

PADMA. For your tea? She's gone in to get it.

BHAU. She must have gone in as soon as she saw me coming. What a sweet girl she is!

PADMA. Yes.

BHAU. What's that supposed to mean?

PADMA. She is.

BHAU. Sometimes you shout at her for no reason at all. She's still a child really.

PADMA. All right.

BHAU. You must show her more consideration.

PADMA. Are you going to lecture me as usual for an hour now? I'm fed up.

   Leelu comes in with a cup of tea.

BHAU. Is that for me, my little one?

LEELU. Yes.

BHAU. And for Aai?

LEELU (*harshly to Padma*). Do you want some?

PADMA. Why should she ask me?

LEELU. Do you want tea?

PADMA. Is there some left?

LEELU. Just tell me if you want some.

PADMA. But . . .

LEELU. What's all this fuss for? Just tell me if you want some.

PADMA. Is Raja back?

LEELU. No.

PADMA. Then I'll have tea with him. It's lonely for him to have it alone.

LEELU (*smouldering*). I won't make tea for him.

PADMA. Listen to her. See what I mean? And you think I'm being unfair. She's always spoiling for a fight. Who asked you to make his tea? I'll make it for him.

LEELU. Make it. Have fun making it. (*Marches out.*)

PADMA. She hates Raja. Is that the way to behave for a girl her age?

BHAU. She gets irritable sometimes. She has so much work in the house.

PADMA. What work? That poor boy is so quiet, you hardly know if he's in or out. Such a well-behaved boy, well brought up, neat, disciplined. Two hundred miles away from his parents for his education. Shouldn't we be kind to him?

BHAU. Why? Who is he to us?

PADMA. Do people have to be related to us by blood for us to be kind to them? Wasn't your son alone once, far away from us? Why don't you think about how lonely he must have got? This chap's a paying guest and we treat him as decently as we should under the circumstances.

PADMA. Decently? When he's like one of the family?

BHAU. Actually, all this was quite unnecessary.

PADMA. He's so sensitive. Have you ever bothered to look at him or get to know him? You're at the office the whole day. And he's too scared of you to come out before you. I've taken care of him however. And it's only now, after four months here, that he's beginning to open up a bit.

BHAU. I wasn't keen on having a paying guest in the first place. These fifty-odd rupees weren't going to make us any richer.

PADMA. But was money the reason we wanted him here?

BHAU. We won't have one next year.

PADMA. There's still time to think about that.

Leelu comes in.

LEELU (*to Padma*). Your pill.

PADMA. Leave it there.

LEELU. It's five o'clock.

PADMA. I said leave it there.

BHAU. But why can't you take it now that she's brought it?

LEELU. She has to hurt me, that's why!

BHAU. Leelu.

PADMA. Get me some water. (*Leelu goes off.*) Let's stop these pills.

BHAU. Now what's wrong?

PADMA. Nothing is wrong. That is why I want to stop them.

BHAU. Don't be a fool. You must complete the course now that you've started it.

PADMA. I'm fed up. And in any case, there's nothing wrong with me.

BHAU. Let's not go into all that again. Just finish the course.

PADMA. I see. So I must finish the course since I started it.

BHAU. God! It's difficult these days to talk to you, even about simple things.

PADMA. Do I insist that you talk to me? Do you know why I want Raja in the house? He's the only one who cares to talk to me of his own accord, with sincerity. That's why. Or else between the two of you you'd have driven me mad with your indifference. How should I pass my days? Tell me how. How?

BHAU. Don't bark at me like that.

PADMA. Take care what you say. How dare you call me a dog?

BHAU. Padma!

Leelu comes in with water.

LEELU. May I go out for a while, Bhau?

BHAU. Ask your mother, my pet.

LEELU. I'm going out.

PADMA (*suddenly furious*). You're not going out. (*Leelu ignores her.*) Leelu!

BHAU. Leelu . . .

LEELU (*throws herself into a chair*). But why not? Why can't I go out?

BHAU. Ask your mother, my pet.

PADMA. You're not going out.

BHAU. Ask her, my love. You must respect your elders. (*Leelu exits, seething. Bhau, shouting at Padma*) Why did you yell at her?

PADMA. Why is she so stubborn? Why does she take such joy in humiliating me?

BHAU. So you yell.

PADMA. Maybe I was wrong. Please don't get angry. (*Uneasy.*) Yes, I was wrong. I know I was. (*Pause.*) I don't know what gets into me. I just lose control. (*Pause.*) Didn't I tell you? We must stop those pills. (*Tearful.*) She must be fed up with me. I know she must. But honestly, I don't mean ill. Never. Don't you think my heart doesn't go out to her? (*Pause.*) She'll never know. Oh God, what is going to become of me?

BHAU. Would you like to lie down a bit? (*Padma shakes her head.*) What is it then? Is your back troubling you again? Padma. . .

PADMA (*overwhelmed with grief*). It's Shashi's twenty-third birthday today. Doesn't anybody remember? Anybody at all?

BHAU. Padma . . .

PADMA. How strange that everybody should have forgotten him.

BHAU. Padma, Padma . . .

PADMA. But I can't forget him.

BHAU. Padma, you must keep a hold on yourself. You will, won't you? Remember what you said? Remember?

PADMA. Yes, I do. I remember. Everything. He went like a lion, fighting. I'm proud of him. That's what I said. But that was a lie. All of it. I want my son back. In any state. I want him back. (*She sobs aloud and then gradually grows quiet.*) Why can't I forget him? I try so hard. (*Pause.*) And now I've messed things up as usual. I'd decided not to talk about him. But I couldn't help it. I get on your nerves, don't I? I must be annoying everybody. I yelled at Leelu. I shouldn't have done that. How can I make her understand? She's not interested in listening to me. I offered to wash her hair the other day and . . . (*Gradually loses herself.*) On Diwali, Shashi would insist on my giving him his oil bath, grown man that he was. Right till the end. I used to yell at him too . . . Oh dear, I mustn't think of him, must I? But I won't cry. He's gone. His time was up. Gone. He used to come marching into the house, his boots clicking smartly, remember? Boisterous, chaotic. His room always a mess, as if a tempest had blown through it . . . How I used to yell at him. What would he have looked like today . . . at twenty-three . . . Rekha's engaged, did you know that? Someone in Indore. She used to buzz around Shashi like a bee when he was home. Everybody avoids me now. I met her mother the other day . . . She barely smiled at me . . . Do I look very ugly? Old? I do, don't I? Don't I? I'm sure I do. Yes, I know it. I don't mind. All I want now is for Leelu to settle down with someone good. Then we could go away. Couldn't we? Give up this house and go? Hunh? Couldn't we?

BHAU. Yes.

PADMA. Yes. Once you've decided not to cross me, you'll never cross me. That's it, isn't it? How long will you care for me in this way? There are times I feel very guilty. Give that coat to me. I'll hang it up. I don't do a thing for you these days. Would you like some more tea? Don't pay any attention to me. You think of Shashi too, don't you? I know you do. You keep everything bottled up inside. Leelu, could you come here for a minute please? Please explain everything to her. Tell her . . . that I don't mean ill. (*Leelu enters.*) Leelu, sweetheart, will you just hang this coat up in the wardrobe? (*Leelu hangs up the coat.*) Come and sit. (*Leelu remains standing.*) Sit down, my love. Please sit down.

BHAU. Sit down, Leelu.

Leelu sits down.

PADMA. She's still angry with me. Talk to Bhau while I get both of you some tea.

LEELU. Not for me, thanks.

PADMA. I'm going to make some.

LEELU. I don't want any.

BHAU. Have some, Leelu.

LEELU. No.

PADMA. Didn't I tell you that she's still angry with me? Well, drink the tea that your Aai has made for you, and I'm sure you'll be angry no longer. (*She goes in to make tea.*)

BHAU. Were you crying? (*Leelu shakes her head.*) No point denying it. I can tell by your eyes.

LEELU. Bhau . . .

BHAU. You're a silly girl.

LEELU. Bhau . . .

BHAU. Yes?

LEELU. Am I really rude?

BHAU. Who says so?

LEELU. I just don't know how to behave with Aai.*

BHAU. You must be very patient and very tolerant.

LEELU. If I don't talk, she flies into a rage.

BHAU. We have to look after her. She doesn't sleep well, you know that.

LEELU. But Bhau, these days she wouldn't take her pills—her medicines. She neglects herself. A couple of times she threw the pills out of the window. How can she ever get well?

BHAU. Please. Let's not talk about any of these things today. She'll remember Shashi and start crying again. Why are you upset? Do you often think of him?

LEELU. Of course. It's only two years since he. . .

BHAU. The house was like bedlam when he was around. Doors banging, him singing, the two of you quarrelling . . .

*Mother, in Marathi.

LEELU. He used to pull my plait so hard. 'Leelu, make some tea. Leelu, get me some water.' And I'd snap back, 'Who do you think I am? Your servant? I won't do anything for you.' Bhau, look at me . . .

BHAU. We must look after Aai. She's become very sensitive.

LEELU. Yes.

BHAU. There's a good girl.

LEELU. Bhau, do you like me?

BHAU. What the hell does that mean, Leelu . . .

LEELU. Do you?

BHAU. Leelya . . .

LEELU. Please tell me, Bhau, do you like me?

BHAU. Yes.

LEELU. As much as Shashi-dada?

BHAU. Parents don't make differences between their children, sweetheart. Come here.

Leelu sits on the floor near Bhau and puts her head in his lap.

LEELU. Bhau . . .

BHAU. Yes, my pet?

LEELU. Bhau, I'd like to tell you something.

BHAU. What?

LEELU. I like you so much.

BHAU. Great! That's excellent news.

LEELU. I mean it, Bhau . . .

BHAU. Leelya, I've made up my mind about something. I'm not going to let you get married. I want you to stay with me always.

LEELU. Suits me. I don't want to get married.

BHAU. Take care, someone might hear you. I've thought of something better. You can get married but I'll ask my son-in-law to live with us. I'll tell him: Our darling daughter isn't prepared to leave us and go with you.

LEELU. God. I'd like to see his face when you tell him that. It'll be a scream.

BHAU. Cheeky twit. That's no way to talk about your husband.

LEELU. But Bhau, I'm not yet . . .

BHAU. Oh, I am looking for one. Looking for one very, very carefully. I've even ordered binoculars. The gem has to be examined thoroughly.

LEELU. But didn't you say just now that you'll not let me marry ever?

BHAU. That was a joke. You are going to have a grand wedding. Hundreds of guests, feasts galore, a mad hubbub all around. And Leelya looks shyly and slyly at the groom, and he, the rogue, enjoys every minute, smiling to himself.

LEELU. Ugh.

BHAU. And I won't let you shed a single tear during the ceremony. I can't stand people snivelling at weddings. Leelya, how many sarees do you want? Tell me quick: Which colours shall we buy? I'll send the order to Banaras right away.

Padma enters with tea.

PADMA. Silk sarees? For whom? Why did she jump up all on a sudden? Lord, seems I have spoilt a tête-à-tête between father and daughter. Have your tea anyway. Silk sarees for whom?

BHAU. We were just joking.

PADMA. So you don't want to tell me?

BHAU. Don't be silly. I was just asking Leelya how many silk sarees she'd like to have for her wedding.

PADMA. Oh yes, of course. How silly of me. I should have known nobody was planning to buy silk sarees for a hag like me . . .

BHAU. Who said so? Of course we'll buy one for you. The one you have now is too old in any case.

PADMA (*suddenly flaring up*). Don't you know on what occasion silk sarees are bought? (*Calming down.*) Have your tea. Leelu, drink your tea. It'll get cold.

BHAU. Come on, Leelu.

Leelu sits still.

PADMA. She won't. Because I've made it.

Raja comes home.

BHAU. Has she said anything? Has she uttered a word?

PADMA. Raja, dear. Come and have this cup of tea. You've come just in time.

BHAU. Raja, would you like to make yourself another cup? That is Leelu's tea.

RAJA (*stammering*). N . . . n . . . no. I mean, I don't want any. Just had some.

LEELU. Take it. I don't want it.

RAJA. B . . . But I've just had some. In the canteen.

PADMA. Take it. How can you say no to a cup of tea at home? Even if Shashi had been to ten different places, once he got home he had to have his home brew. Come, take it.

LEELU. I don't want it. I don't want that tea. (*Harshly*) I don't want it.

PADMA. Don't pay any attention to her. She's always like that.

BHAU. Was there any need to hurt her now?

PADMA. I didn't say anything to her. She doesn't care much for tea anyway. And she's always looking for excuses to get angry.

BHAU. I don't want that tea either.

PADMA. Now you don't get upset. The world hasn't come to an end. She'll forget. (*Pause.*) And if she's in a fury of sulking, let her be. Here everyone can be angry and offended. But I alone am denied that right. (*Pause.*) Even when there's talk going on of buying silk sarees on the birthday of a lost son.

BHAU. What's the time? Will someone tell me the time? Raja, what's the time?

PADMA. There's no need to change the subject in such a hurry. I'm not going to shout or cry.

BHAU. It's not for that. I want to go to the club.

PADMA. Must you go, even today?

BHAU. What's the use of sitting at home? Actually, why don't you come along too? It'll do you a world of good.

RAJA. Shall I g . . . go to my room?

BHAU (*faintly annoyed*). Go if you want to. You don't need to ask for permission. You've had your tea? Haven't you?

PADMA. Keep sitting, dear. No, I can't make it to the club today. My back is bad. I'd rather sit talking to Raja.

BHAU. Suit yourself. I'll be back by ten.

PADMA. Come when you like.

BHAU. Don't wait dinner for me.

PADMA. No. (*Bhau leaves.*) As if I'm going to have dinner today.

RAJA. Aren't you well?

PADMA. Yes and no. Just a feeling.

RAJA. I asked because you said you weren't going to eat.

PADMA. Hunh.

RAJA. Are you fasting? Of course you must be. It's Saturday, isn't it?

PADMA. Raja, you silly boy, when have you seen me fasting on a Saturday?

RAJA. Then . . .

PADMA. Don't bother about me. You have your dinner with Leelu.

RAJA. You must eat with us, please.

PADMA. You want me to?

RAJA. Yes.

PADMA. See? No one would say a thing like that to me in this house. How old are you, Raja?

RAJA. Sixteen, Kaku.

PADMA. There. That's the umpteenth time I've asked you. Sixteen, are you? You're a grown-up man, Raja.

RAJA. And yet you pamper me like a little boy.

PADMA. Do I pamper you?

RAJA. I think you do.

PADMA. How do you feel about that? Good or bad?

RAJA. It makes me feel at home.

PADMA. I don't pamper you all that much, do I ?

RAJA. You tidy up my room, insist on my having a second helping at dinner, and . . . and other things like that.

PADMA. I hope I don't annoy you. (*Raja clicks his tongue.*) That's no way to say no. You're just a little baby. Raja, you must think of this as your home.

---

*Paternal aunt, in Marathi. Also a common form of address for an older woman.

Don't you dare think of moving to another place next year. I'll feel very hurt if you do.

RAJA. But, Kaku, why don't you charge me?

PADMA. Now I'll get really angry with you.

RAJA. But it makes me feel very awkward. I wish you'd take some money from me, or I'll tell Bhau.

PADMA. Now, now, Raja. He must never get to know about it. This is your home. Is it not? Tell me it is. Isn't it?

RAJA (*reluctantly*). Yes.

PADMA. You mean it?

RAJA. Yes.

PADMA. Swear by me.

RAJA. Kaku. . . .

PADMA. Swear. Put your hand to my throat. That's it. (*She forces his hand to her throat.*) Now say: This house is my home. This is my home. (*Raja quickly withdraws his hand.*) You don't feel anything for me, I know it.

RAJA. But, Kaku . . .

PADMA. Dear, dear Raja, you will never understand this deep, deep affection that we women feel. If your mother comes here some day, I'll tell her: Give me your son, I'd like to adopt him.

RAJA. She'll never agree.

PADMA. Why not?

RAJA. Because she loves me so much. I can't tell you how much.

PADMA. Don't I?

RAJA. Of course you do. But she's different. After all, she's my mother.

PADMA (*bitterly*). That's true.

RAJA. Both times when I left home to come here, she wept.

PADMA. I'm sure she did.

RAJA. But I told her. . .

PADMA. Did you also weep?

RAJA. Yes, I did. Not too much. A little.

PADMA. Poor woman. She must have wondered what kind of a wilderness her darling son was going to.

RAJA. No, you're wrong, I'd told her about you.

PADMA. Raja . . .

RAJA. I really did.

PADMA. Raja, I don't want to meet your mother.

RAJA. But you just said you . . .

PADMA. God forbid. Seeing me, your mother might wonder what kind of an ogress her dear son's been trapped by . . .

RAJA. Never.

PADMA. And she'll grab him away from me.

RAJA. Kaku, you say the funniest things at times.

PADMA. Won't she feel that way? You don't know it. But I can never keep and enjoy anything good that comes my way.

RAJA. You'll never believe how good my mother is.

PADMA. And I am terrible, aren't I? An ogress, like I said just now.

RAJA. Kaku, why do you suddenly become so depressed?

PADMA. Raja, I want to know the truth. Please tell me: Do you think I'm a good woman?

RAJA. Yes.

PADMA (*taking his hand*). Swear.

RAJA (*freeing his hand*). Kaku, I don't like this swearing business all the time.

PADMA. Because it's me you don't like. No one really likes me. I'm a hopeless woman. Arrey, you don't have to feel so bad about it. See . . . does Leelu like me? She can't bear to be anywhere near me. And he's gone now. One mustn't go on remembering. But I can't help it. He was always out. Games. Friends. And then of course he had to join the army. Raja, if you don't like it, I'll not talk any more. But please don't leave this house. Please don't go. It's a large house. You need people to fill it. Without people, where's its charm? How enonnous they've made it! If Shashi had been alive, he alone would have filled it with his vitality, with his presence. It was his luck to stay in a small flat of three rooms. He'd always say: Aai, I'm too big for this flat. Let's build a proper house. And I'd say: You fool, don't we need money for that? Can houses be built just by wishing? The house was built eventually. With his money too. But he is gone.

RAJA. Kaku . . .

PADMA. Hunh. Oh dear, I've been talking too much again.

RAJA. Was Shashi like you?

PADMA. In looks he was like his father, but his nature was just like mine. Easily hurt. But he'd never show it. It would burn him up inside. I'll tell you what happened when he decided to join the anny. I said to him: Why do you want to leave us and go so far away? Why don't you become a doctor or an engineer? THe never said a word. Not that he was annoyed or was curt to us. He just used to be very, very quiet. Gloomy. Sad. Finally I thought: He's my own child after all, let him have his way. (*Trembling.*) Well, he had his stubborn way!

RAJA. I want to become a doctor.

PADMA. Is that so? Have you taken biology?

RAJA. Yes. I like the medical profession.

PADMA. That's right, my child. You must become a doctor. It'll be a good thing for me. When there's a doctor in the house, you don't have to go running around in emergencies.

RAJA. Is your back aching today?

PADMA. Yes, dear. My back, my head. It goes on.

RAJA. You were taking some pills, weren't you?

PADMA. What's the point? Pills do nothing. Do you think these doctors know what they are about? They don't even diagnose a complaint correctly. They pretend to examine you here and there, scribble a prescription and then take twenty-five rupees. You ask them why there's no improvement, and they tell you your mind is weak. Let your mind grow strong and you'll improve. If I can do that, then why do I require these good-for-nothing doctors? I've given up taking these pills.

RAJA. But that will make you feel worse.

PADMA. What difference will it make? How many days do I have left in any case?

RAJA. Why? You're . . . not old.

PADMA. Aren't I?

RAJA. Rot.

PADMA. Tell me: How old do you think I am?

RAJA (*instinctively lying*). Thirty-seven or thirty-eight at the most.

PADMA (*happily*). Forty. (*Embarrassed by her own falsehood*) Actually, I've just crossed forty. But I look fiftyish, don't I?

RAJA. Your hair's greying a bit, that's all.

PADMA (*hiding her irritation*). That has nothing to do with age. It started going grey soon after Shashi's birth. Giving birth is like being born again, my dear. And Shashi was no puny baby. That was when my hair started to fall. You should have seen my hair before that. You won't believe it if I tell you. When I sat on a stool, my hair would sweep the floor behind me. (*Laughing coyly.*) I was quite a beauty in my youth, you know. (*Raja smiles awkwardly.*) You can't believe it, can you? I can hardly believe it myself when I look in the mirror. Look at my hair now. And my complexion. In those days, my hands used to be sheer silk, like rose petals. They look terrible now, don't they?

RAJA. Of course not.

PADMA. Hard and bony.

RAJA. Uh-huh.

PADMA. I'll show you my old photographs. Then you'll know what I was like. They are lovely. There's one of me in a chair and Bhau on the arm of the chair. It was taken soon after our marriage. Then there's one in which I'm doing puja, wearing a gold-embroidered silk saree and all my jewellery. You'd never think that was me.

RAJA. We have some pretty funny photos of my mother as well. One with her wearing jewellery made out of white sugar balls, another with jewellery made out of flowers and her on a swing. Aai's written a caption underneath: Flower Queen. Baba added 'pregnant' in brackets. How we laugh when we see those pictures!

PADMA (*faintly annoyed*). My pictures aren't funny like that. (*Pause.*) I did look really lovely those days.

RAJA (*conscious of the gaffe he's made*). But you still look very nice, Kaku.

PADMA. You're cheeky, aren't you, saying things like that to me!

RAJA. But it's the truth . . .

PADMA. Now if you'd said something like that to a girl in your class . . . why are you blushing?

RAJA. Who said I am?

PADMA. You do talk to the girls in your class, don't you?

RAJA. Never.

PADMA. Why ever not?

RAJA. Oh, Kaku! What questions you ask!

PADMA. Why? You're sixteen now, aren't you? That's old enough. Any day now you're going to fall in love. (*Raja squirms.*) Or have you already?

RAJA. Please, Kaku, let's talk of something else.

PADMA. Why? Because you have fallen in love. Haven't you? Haven't you?

RAJA. Let me go, Kaku.

PADMA. Raja.

RAJA. I must study.

PADMA. Don't be angry, dear. I was only joking.

RAJA. What sort of a joke is that?

PADMA. Oh, all right. I'm sorry. We'll talk very seriously now. Please sit down. Please.

RAJA. But I have so much homework to do.

PADMA (*laughing*). Oh, your homework! I know what it is. It's reading that magazine that's kept under the pillow. Have I guessed right? (*Laughs outright.*) Dear, dear Raja. You shouldn't be reading that kind of stuff at your age.

RAJA. B . . . but it doesn't belong to me.

PADMA. How does that matter? I found it under your bed.

RAJA (*suddenly angry*). Kaku, please don't tidy up my room in future.

PADMA. Why?

RAJA. I don't want you to.

PADMA. Why not? You've brought more of those magazines, have you?

RAJA. I don't like people messing around in my room when I'm not there.

PADMA. Raja.

RAJA. I'll do my room myself.

PADMA. But I used to do Shashi's room for him.

RAJA. I'd prefer to do my own.

PADMA. What's got into you all of a sudden? You were all right a moment ago. Raja, have I done something wrong? Raja . . . (*Raja starts to leave.*) Here (*grabbing his hand*)—tell me you're not angry any more.

RAJA (*jerking his hand away in annoyance*). I'm not. (*He goes to his room.*)

Padma is restless. Picks up her knitting. Puts it down. Examines her hands. Looks at herself in the mirror. Listens outside Raja's room. Sits down again. After a little while:

PADMA. Leelu! Leelu!

Leelu enters.

LEELU. Now what?

PADMA. What are you doing?

LEELU. Nothing.

PADMA. Why is your hair loose?

LEELU. I was plaiting it.

PADMA. So you were doing something. You should have said you were plaiting your hair. Come. Let me plait it for you.

LEELU. No, thanks. I'd rather do it myself.

PADMA. Nonsense! Look at your hair. All matted up. Get me the comb. (*Leelu sits down without a word.*) Such beautiful hair. Like silk. Turned it into strands of jute. They come out with all these new fads. They even say: Don't oil it. You were plaiting it in the garden, weren't you?

LEELU. No.

PADMA. Then by the door?

LEELU. So what? Yes, I was at the door.

PADMA. But why?

LEELU. Why not? Just like that.

PADMA. How many times have I told you not to do your hair standing in the garden or by the door? A thousand people go up and down the road. Does it look nice?

LEELU. Let them look if they want to.

PADMA. Let them look? You're not a child any more. I'm soon going to stop you wearing those skirts. It'll be sarees for you from now on.

LEELU. Make it nine-yard sarees. Why not?

PADMA. There's no need to get nasty. Those skirts are quite embarrassing at times.

LEELU. They aren't if you're careful.

PADMA. When are you girls ever careful? You told me yourself what happened to Shubha. Silly girl. It would be better to stay at home for three days. (*Pause.*) Did you have any trouble this time?

LEELU. No.

PADMA. Is that the truth?

LEELU. Why should I lie? Besides, I've never had any trouble whatever. It's only your imagination.

PADMA. You girls will never understand how serious it all is. To be a mother . . .

LEELU. That'll do. Please don't give me your usual lecture. We know all about it from our physiology classes at school. Would you please pass me the comb now?

PADMA. What did they teach you?

LEELU. This and that. Why don't you give me the comb? Ugh. Look at those plaits.

PADMA. Just a little tight, that's all. What did they teach you?

LEELU. Why is this bit of hair standing up? Damn . . .

PADMA. Leelu, what did they teach you?

LEELU. For god's sake, Aai. Things that everybody knows. Aai, please buy me a lungi.

PADMA. What for? Why ask me? Ask your father. He's going to buy you a dozen gold-embroidered silk sarees in any case. Some people have no conscience. Forget your father. He's a man after all. But shouldn't you know better? Is this the day to talk about new clothes?

LEELU. What suddenly gets into you, Aai?

PADMA. Oh, you little witch. How could you forget your only brother?

LEELU. Aai, don't call me names, I'm warning you. I think you'd better go and lie down in your room.

PADMA. There's nothing wrong with me.

LEELU. That's obvious. You get like this when your period is delayed.

PADMA (*flaring up*). There's nothing the matter with me. Understand? Nothing. You're all a pack of fools. Including the doctor. (*Pause.*) Ugh. (*Pause.*) It makes me so mad. I don't know what's happening to me . . . Go. Have your dinner, both of you.

LEELU. And you?

PADMA. I'll go and rest for a while.

LEELU. I won't come and ask you again.

PADMA. Call Raja.

LEELU. He'll come if he's hungry. (*Goes in.*)

> *Padma goes to her room. Looks at herself in the mirror. She is restless. She takes some old photographs from the cupboard. Then some sarees and other clothes. Sits with these scattered around her. Raja goes from his room to hers.*

PADMA. Is that Raja? What is it, dear?

RAJA. Nothing in particular. I just . . .

PADMA. Come. Come and sit down.

RAJA. No, thanks. I mean . . .

PADMA. Weren't you supposed to be doing your homework?

RAJA. That magazine of mine . . .

PADMA. What about it?

RAJA. Have . . . Have you got it?

PADMA. No.

RAJA. I wanted to return it. It's not in my room, so I . . .

PADMA. It was right there. You've not looked. Why should I take it?

RAJA. Oh, well.

PADMA. Are you going?

RAJA. Yes.

PADMA. Didn't you say you wanted to see my pictures? Why don't you sit?

RAJA. Are these all your clothes?

PADMA. I should go around showing them to everybody. (*Drapes a folded saree over her shoulders.*) How does it look? The colour?

RAJA. Nice.

PADMA. Raja, what is your favourite colour?

RAJA. M . . . My favourite? Well, blue, I suppose . . . pink.

PADMA. Look at this saree. Isn't this a beautiful blue?

RAJA. Oh yes. And the smell of new clothes is so nice.

PADMA. One must wear pearls with this one. Nothing else will do.

RAJA. Don't you ever wear it, Kaku ?

PADMA (*pushing everything away*). I can't bear it.

RAJA. Are you feeling unwell again?

PADMA. It's my head. (*Pause.*) If only somebody would press it for me. (*Pause.*)

RAJA. Would you like me to ?

PADMA. Uh?

RAJA. Would you like me to press it?

PADMA. Would you?

RAJA. If it'll make you feel better.

PADMA. It will. (*Padma closes her eyes. Raja presses her head.*) How beautifully you do it. You have a lovely hand.

Leelu comes into the sitting room. Then goes to Raja's room. Then stands outside Padma's room, listening. After a moment:

LEELU. Raja . . .

Raja and Padma start. Raja comes out.

RAJA. Did you call me?

They look at each other.

LEELU. Are you planning to eat?

RAJA. So soon? It's just about six.

LEELU. Make up your mind fast.

RAJA. I will if you're going to.

LEELU. Don't do me any favours, please. Eat if you're hungry. And if you're not, say so.

RAJA. Hell, don't get ragged . . . *(Pause.)*

LEELU. What were you doing in Aai's room?

RAJA. Went to see if my mag . . . book was there.

LEELU. Was it?

RAJA. No.

LEELU. What was it?

RAJA. Oh, just something . . .

LEELU. What?

RAJA. Nothing really . . .

LEELU. If you don't want to tell me, say so. I didn't say I didn't want to, did I? Then why don't you tell me? *(Raja goes into his room without answering. Leelu marches angrily in after him.)* Raja, don't you dare be rude to me. I'm warning you. When was I rude? I've been watching you. When I ask you something, you either ignore me, or fob me off with a silly answer. Who the hell do you think you are, anyway? This house is mine, you'd better remember that.

RAJA. I'm not denying it, but . . .

LEELU. The way you go around, anyone would think you're the King of England. You'can't even tidy up your own room.

RAJA. How does that bother you? Kaku tidies it for me.

LEELU. And you don't mind her being put to so much trouble.

RAJA. But she insists . . .

LEELU. She might too. But shouldn't you have a little more brains than to let her?

RAJA. Don't you start talking about my brains, do you understand?

LEELU. I will, ten million times . . .

RAJA. Shall I ask you something?

LEELU. What?

RAJA. Are you jealous of me?

LEELU (*furious*). Wha . . . at?

RAJA. You're jealous, because Kaku pays more attention to me than to you.

LEELU. Shut up. A paying guest is a paying guest. What cheek!.

RAJA. And what do you think you are? Just foodmongers!

LEELU (*shouts*). Raja!

Raja checks himself. After a pause.

RAJA. Sorry.

LEELU. Saying sorry doesn't help. People should think a bit before they speak. (*She is close to tears.*)

RAJA. Listen to me, Leelu . . .

LEELU. Don't talk to me.

RAJA. I didn't mean what I said.

LEELU. Didn't I tell you not to speak to me?

RAJA. But I said I'm sorry, really.

LEELU. You don't have to. In this house, I'm not worth much more than a servant.

RAJA. Please, Leelu. I'm really sorry.

LEELU. Raja.

RAJA. Yes?

LEELU. You must leave.

RAJA. What?

LEELU. You must go away from here. From this house.

RAJA. Where to?

LEELU. Wherever.

RAJA. Why?

LEELU. Don't ask questions. Just go.

RAJA. But why?

LEELU. Didn't I tell you? You'll get a room anywhere.

RAJA. What will Kaku say?

LEELU. That's my problem.

RAJA. Only a little while ago she was telling me I must come back here next year as well.

LEELU. Was she?

RAJA. Yes.

LEELU. No. You must go. Now.

RAJA. I must talk to her.

LEELU. Why do you want to do that? It's because you don't want to leave this place . . .

RAJA. But Kaku would take it very badly.

LEELU. Oh, she's going to be terribly, dreadfully heartbroken! She'll probably go crazy with grief. But you must go. (*Raja thinks hard.*) How can you be so insensitive? Do you think I don't understand things? Have you no self-respect? I've been saying such horrid things to you. How can you stand there and take it all?

RAJA. But you don't mean any of the things you say.

LEELU. Where did you get that bit of insight from?

RAJA. Kaku was telling me not to mind you when you say things like that. She said you get like that because you're overworked.

LEELU. Oh, the hypocrite!

RAJA. How can you say that about your own mother?

LEELU. I'm *only* telling the truth.

RAJA. But a mother is a mother, after all.

LEELU. Your mother must be an epitome of love, one of those ideal ones you get in novels, so you can write another *Shyamchi Aai*. Sissy.

RAJA. There's nothing sissy about talking lovingly of your mother.

LEELU. But you are a sissy. Our Shashi-dada wasn't a bit like that.

RAJA. There's no need to compare me with anybody.

LEELU. I'm only telling you because Aai keeps saying a hundred times over, 'He's like Shashi to me, he's like Shashi to me.' Well, you're not. See?

RAJA. But I never said I am.

LEELU. Nobody can take Shashi-dada's place.

RAJA. I don't claim to.

LEELU. You can't. There is no way you can. (*Viciously.*) He never was a sissy like you. He was huge. Six feet tall. Kept hitting his head against the top of the doorway. And what a sportsman. He won university colours. When he laughed, the walls would tremble. And the hundreds of friends he had. And you? The minute classes are over, you follow your nose straight back home. (*Raja is hurt, Leelu is happy to have found her mark. Raja is demoralized.*)

RAJA. I'll go away. (*Pause.*)

LEELU (*softening*). You don't have to go right away. You can stay till the first.

RAJA. I'll go back to my village.

LEELU. And what about your classes?

RAJA. I'll miss them.

LEELU (*aggressive*). And blame me for making you miss them.

RAJA. You have nothing to do with it.

LEELU. Huh. (*Pause.*) You don't have to go and report all this to Aai.

RAJA. I don't feel happy here.

LEELU (*surprised*). Don't like college?

RAJA. No, I don't.

LEELU (*giggling*). Gosh! (*Pause. Feeling sorry for him.*) You keep too much to yourself. That's why. How can you feel happy that way? I've been watching you. Everybody's busy having fun in the canteen or out on the lawns, but you're in the library.

RAJA. I like reading.

LEELU. That's all very well. But a chap's got to have friends. I wouldn't survive a day without friends.

RAJA. I forget everything when I start reading.

LEELU. Yes, Mr Scholar. That's what my friends call you. There's Mr Scholar, they say. There's Mr Scholar.

RAJA. They all laugh at me, I suppose.

LEELU. Don't they just! But that's normal. There's nobody we don't laugh at.

RAJA. Hey, Leelu . . .

LEELU. Yes, Mr Rajaram . . .

RAJA. I want to ask you something if you promise not to make fun of me.

LEELU. Tell me.

RAJA. There. I can tell from your voice that you're already laughing at me.

LEELU. Come on. Don't be so touchy. Ask.

RAJA. I can't now.

LEELU. Come on. I promise I won't make fun of you.

RAJA. You mean it?

LEELU. Yes.

RAJA (*after a pause*). Forget it.

LEELU. God, what a twit you are! Come on, Ask.

RAJA. Ah . . . um . . . (*Laughs in embarrassment.*)

LEELU. Dear god, now what . . .

RAJA (*very quickly, in one breath*). I look like an oaf and a country bumpkin, don't I?

Leelu laughs outright.

LEELU. What a prize question after that prologue!

RAJA. Please tell me.

LEELU. What?

RAJA. What I asked you. Don't I look like an oaf?

LEELU (*mock seriously*). Certainly not. With all those hep clothes you got made the very day you came here. What more does one need? The only problem is the buckle on your belt. It tends to slip to the right of centre. And your shirt hangs out at the back. . . otherwise you're fine, just fine.

RAJA. Really? Why didn't you tell me?

LEELU. And spoil all our fun? Huh. And those shoes of yours. What have you got nailed to the soles? What a clatter you make when you walk.

RAJA. Do I?

LEELU. Don't tell me you've never noticed. That day when you walked down the corridor, we could hear you till the very end of it. The professor stopped his lecture and said . . .

RAJA. What did he say?

LEELU. Nothing.

RAJA. Please tell me, please.

LEELU. You'll feel bad.

RAJA. Look here, Leelu . . .

LEELU. Won't you feel bad?

RAJA. No, I won't.

LEELU (*giggling*). He said, 'The rustic fool.'

RAJA. Huh.

LEELU. How we laughed. He's very funny. We were all laughing, so he says to us, 'Right. Tell me what rustic means.' And we laughed some more.

RAJA. Did you know what it meant?

LEELU. Of course I didn't. But one always laughs when others laugh.

RAJA. Rustic means country bumpkin.

LEELU. There, you're feeling bad. Didn't I say you would?

RAJA. Leelu, I'll never be smart like city people. What terrific English they speak.

LEELU. But they flunk in the exams. These English-medium types are all like that. They're fine to listen to. But ask them to spell 'take' and they spell it 'tek'. Everybody was knocked out cold when they heard what you'd scored in the terminals.

RAJA. But you've got to be able to speak English well.

LEELU. I'm not denying that. It's just a matter of practice, really. We don't take enough pains over it, that's all.

RAJA. Don't you also feel that people will laugh if you make a mistake?

LEELU. Listen. I have a brainwave . . . Why don't we talk to each other in English at home? There's nobody to laugh at us.

RAJA. But aren't I supposed to leave this place?

LEELU. Oh, shut up. Tell me: What is your name?

RAJA. Great! What a great beginning!

LEELU. Don't be snooty. Everybody knows about your making the merit list in your school cert.

RAJA. I'm not snooty. Do I ever put on airs?

LEELU. Not really. But people think you're snooty because you're so reserved. Is that how you'll be with your patients when you become a doctor?

RAJA. A doctor doesn't need to chat his head off.

LEELU. Biology must be quite tough. All those frogs to cut up. Ugh!

RAJA. What's ugh about that? Later we'll cut up corpses.

LEELU. Eek! I'd just faint.

RAJA. Perhaps you'd enjoy botany. That's a clean subject . . .

LEELU. Does that have to do with all those flowers you keep tearing to shreds with that skewer?

RAJA. It's called a needle, not a skewer. You have to take flowers apart to find out how they are made up.

LEELU. Is it very difficult?

RAJA. Rot. Even you'll understand. Shall I teach you?

LEELU. Huh!

The room fills gradually with the golden light of evening.

RAJA. Here. Look at this flower. This stalk is called the pedicel. The green covering of leaves around the petals is the calyx. These are the petals. This here is the corolla. And these rods in here, these are called the stamens. These are the anthers. Androecium. Now hold on a moment. (*Cuts open the flower vertically with the needle. Leelu draws in her breath.*) Here. This part is called the antherlobe. It contains grains of pollen. Now this produces two gametes, that is, the male seeds. This here is the ovary. Can you see what's in there? Can you? Well, those are the ovules. They contain the female gametes. These fuse to form the zygote. Out of this fusion comes the embryo. Isn't it easy? Nothing to it.

LEELU. Uh-huh.

RAJA. I don't know why people think these subjects are difficult.

LEELU. Raja . . .

RAJA. H'm?

LEELU. Shall I tell you something?

RAJA. Yes?

LEELU (*giggling behind her hand*). I didn't understand a thing.

RAJA. Nonsense.

LEELU. Honest.

RAJA. Shall I tell you again ?

LEELU. I don't mind. You teach rather well.

RAJA. Meaning?

LEELU. You have a lovely voice. Kind of deep and resonant. And how involved you were in what you were saying.

RAJA. Leelu . . .

LEELU. Hunh.

RAJA. Oh, nothing.

LEELU. Please tell me.

RAJA. Do you think I'll make a successful doctor?

LEELU. Of course you will. And filthy rich too.

RAJA. I don't care for that.

LEELU. What then?

RAJA. Money isn't my aim.

LEELU. Then?

RAJA. Leelu, there's such poverty in our country. How do you feel about all those miserable people?

LEELU. I feel terribly sorry for them.

RAJA. Yes. You feel a deep pity for them. You feel their not having money will one day mean death for them. And then you say to yourself: What use is all my education?

LEELU. I know.

RAJA. You agree, don't you? There are people who laugh when I say such things.

LEELU. Why go around talking to people like that?

RAJA. I thought you'd laugh too.

LEELU. Is that what you think of me?

RAJA. It's not that. It was just a feeling. But I'll tell you everything from now on. You know what I'm going to do? Start my practice in a village. I want to be with those people twenty-four hours of the day.

LEELU. Won't you marry?

RAJA. Uh?

LEELU. Oh, nothing.

RAJA. No, I won't. I don't want anything to interfere with my aim.

LEELU. Suppose you fall in love?

RAJA. Go on. That'll never happen.

LEELU. You can never say.

RAJA. Then I will. I'll marry if I fall in love. She'll also be a doctor, and we'll work together.

LEELU. I had no idea you felt this way about things.

RAJA. This way?

LEELU. You're so noble. I had no idea . . .

RAJA. Aw! Come on.

LEELU. I love idealists.

RAJA. Leelu.

LEELU. Um?

RAJA. Leelu . . .

LEELU. Um?

RAJA. Oh, nothing.

LEELU. Raja.

RAJA. Yes?

LEELU. What were you going to say?

RAJA. Nothing.

LEELU. Raja, are we doing something wrong?

RAJA. Why?

LEELU. I think we were talking a lot of rubbish. About love and things like that.

RAJA. What's wrong with that? We were just talking.

LEELU. Raja, sometimes I feel so unhappy.

RAJA. Why?

LEELU. Nothing I can put my finger on. But I want to open up and cry.

RAJA. Yes. I feel that way at times. Sad and depressed. (*Pause.*)

RAJA. Leelu . . .

LEELU. Um?

RAJA. That thing I was going to say . . .

LEELU. Yes?

RAJA. Will you get mad at me if I tell you?

LEELU. No.

RAJA. I'd . . . I'd brought the . . . this flower . . . for you. (*Pause.*)

LEELU. Really?

RAJA. In fact I bring one every day. But I'm so scared to give it to you.

LEELU. Yes?

RAJA. Is that wrong? (*Pause.*)

LEELU. Raja, are we committing a sin?

RAJA. Are we?

LEELU. Suppose what we're doing is bad?

RAJA. Um.

LEELU. Don't feel bad about it, Raja.

RAJA. No.

LEELU. Promise you won't feel bad.

RAJA. No.

LEELU. So we'll be friends, won't we?

RAJA. Yes. (*Pause.*)

LEELU. Can I go now?

RAJA. Must you?

LEELU. But we'll meet again.

RAJA. Oh, all right.

LEELU (*at the door*). Raja . . .

RAJA. Um.

LEELU. I hope you'll forget what you were saying.

RAJA. About what?

LEELU. About looking for another room. (*Pause.*) I wasn't myself when I said that. (*Pause.*) OK?

RAJA. OK.

Leelu leaves. Padma enters wearing the Banarasi silk saree.

PADMA (*embarrassed, nervous, heady laugh*). What are you doing? Studying?

RAJA. No.

PADMA. I've worn it. Because you asked me why I never wear these sarees.

RAJA. Oh!

PADMA. Does it look nice?

RAJA. Yes.

PADMA. People will think I've gone mad. But I had to wear it because of what you said. (*Pause.*) Why are you looking so nervous?

RAJA. No, no, nothing.

The room slowly darkens with the gathering dusk.

PADMA. There's something the matter with me. I'm wearing such a saree but somehow I don't feel happy about it. Raja, it's a terrible thing to grow old. One should always stay young. You're sixteen, aren't you? Just turned sixteen? There's a faint moustache on your upper lip. In a couple of years you'll begin to shave. Silly child. Why are you blushing? When Shashi started, he closed all the doors and windows of his room and scraped his cheeks raw.

RAJA (*uncomfortable*). Kaku, do you mind if we sit out there?

PADMA. Why? (*Pause.*)

RAJA. It's hot in here.

PADMA. Is it?

RAJA. Yes.

PADMA. I think this is fine. In your room. I'd rather stay here. (*Pointing to the bed*) May I sit? Lie down a bit?

RAJA. If you want to.

Leelu enters the drawing room. Listens. Then quickly enters Padma's room. Spots the bundle of letters lying there. She hesitates for a moment, then picks it up. Comes back to the drawing room and looks through them. And becomes deeply upset.

PADMA. Raja . . .

RAJA. Um?

PADMA. I'm a very unhappy woman.

RAJA. Because Shashi is dead?

PADMA. You probably ask yourself why Kaku behaves so oddly.

RAJA. Oh, no, never.

PADMA (*to herself*). But I don't understand myself. Am I wrong or are the others wrong? How should I behave? I don't seem to find anything interesting. Nothing attracts me. I keep wondering what I'm doing, and for what or for whom. (*Raja switches on the light.*) Why did you do that?

RAJA. It's dark.

PADMA. Switch it off.

RAJA. But it's dark . . .

PADMA. Switch it off. (*Raja switches off the light.*) I feel better in the dark. It's so restful. This dark. Don't you feel that way? (*Pause.*) Raja, I think I'm starting to get a temperature.

RAJA. Shall I call the doctor?

PADMA. What use would he be? I'd rather you sat here near me. I'd feel much better.

RAJA (*very comfortable*). Shall I call Leelu?

PADMA (*with an edge to her voice*). What for?

RAJA. She was just telling me . . .

PADMA. Was she here for a chat?

RAJA. Well, yes . . . in the sense it was I who said to her . . .

PADMA. What were you two talking about? (*Pause.*) Raja, this won't do. You must study. You can't afford to waste time chatting.

RAJA. It was only for a little while.

PADMA. Even that's not necessary. (*Pause.*) Are you angry?

RAJA. May I switch the light on?

PADMA. But why? The light, the light. I'm not going to devour you. Can't you see my eyes hurt in bright light? (*Pause.*) Raja!

RAJA. Um.

PADMA. I'm sure I've got temperature. And it's going to go really high. How hot my forehead is! Just feel it.

Raja doesn't move. Then he gets up and switches on the light. Padma looks hurt. Bhau enters the drawing room.

BHAU. Hullo, my Lillikins. Not studying.? (*Leelu shakes her head.*) Have you had your dinner? (*Leelu shakes her head.*) Why? I've told you again and again not to wait dinner for me. Where's Padma?

Leelu doesn't answer. Padma enters. Both Bhau and Leelu are stunned.

PADMA. Why are you looking at me like that? As if you'd seen a ghost. I know exactly what's going on in your minds. Look at her, all decked out in silks after the fuss she made! (*Pause.*) But I've decided to do as you say. I'm not going to lose myself in grief. I'll pretend he's still alive. That's why I've worn this. You're not angry, are you?

BHAU. Why should I be angry?

PADMA. Well, I just thought . . .

BHAU. You must do what pleases you. You mustn't worry about us.

PADMA. I'm just a silly old woman. You must look after me.

BHAU. Have you had dinner?

PADMA. You eat.

BHAU. And you?

PADMA. I don't feel like it. (*Going towards her room*) Could you, could you come in here for a moment?

Bhau goes with her. Leelu goes to Raja's room.

LEELU. Bastard.

RAJA. Hey. Why? What happened?

Leelu looks at him with hatred.

LEELU (*shrieking*). Get out of here.

The stage is dark. A spot picks out Bhau and Padma.

BHAU. Why did you have to choose today to go through all this junk?

PADMA. I was miserable. I thought these old photos would cheer me up.

BHAU. I'd forgotten about these photos.

PADMA. You've forgotten a lot of things.

BHAU. What does that mean?

PADMA. That you have a wife, for instance. That she is beautiful. Or at least was. That she might have desires, expectations. You've forgotten all that.

BHAU. What would you like me to do about it?

PADMA. Nothing.

BHAU. Then why do you complain?

PADMA. These days even the simplest things I say sound complaining to you.

BHAU. I'll go and have dinner.

PADMA. I asked you to come to my room. You've hardly been here a second and you want to go for dinner?

BHAU. Then why don't you tell me what you want?

PADMA. Oh, nothing.

BHAU. Look here, Padma, I'm very tired. I've been running around all day. And don't think that you're the only one who remembers and you are the only one who grieves.

PADMA. And yet you want to go and have dinner.

BHAU. Have we been starving all these days?

PADMA. Today is different.

BHAU. But didn't you say just now that you've decided not to let your sorrow get you down?

PADMA. That was just bravado. It doesn't last. Please sit near me. Please. (*She flares up as Bhau sits down, expressionless.*) Look, if you can't look any happier than that, there's no need to sit here. I don't want any favours.

BHAU. Why don't you think just a little before you talk? You carry on this way the whole day with that child listening.

PADMA. She's not a child any more.

BHAU. She's only fifteen. This is the time you should be taking great care of her. Instead, she has to look after you.

PADMA. I've heard enough of that. I'm going to ask that Raja to look for a new place.

BHAU. Where does he come in?

PADMA. He doesn't. But it's best this way. They are both the same age.

BHAU. You were all sympathy for him some time ago.

PADMA. Because he is a very nice boy. I have nothing against him.

BHAU. Are you implying that you have something against our daughter?

PADMA. I never said so. But it's a dangerous age. They were chatting away for a whole hour this very evening.

BHAU. If you've decided to tell him to go, suit yourself. It makes no difference to me either way.

PADMA. Why do you brush things off like this?

BHAU. I have full faith in my child.

PADMA. And I? Don't I have faith in her?

BHAU. Are you through?

PADMA. No. There's lots more I want to say.

BHAU. Then get it over with.

PADMA. I'm not happy here.

BHAU. Would you like to visit Raghunath for a few days?

PADMA. What I meant was: I don't feel happy in this new house.

BHAU. You wanted a house of your own.

PADMA. Yes, I did. But I didn't know that my dream was to be realized in this horrible way.

BHAU. That's enough. I don't want another word from you.

PADMA. Why? You find it difficult to take? Don't you? I lose my precious son and you raise a house on his insurance money. Don't you feel any shame? Any shame at all?

BHAU. Padma!

PADMA. You should've given it away. To some charity. You killed my son.

BHAU. Padma!

PADMA. Why didn't you stop him? He was wild. He was thoughtless. Why didn't you stop him when he said he wanted to join the army?

BHAU. Padma, have you ever let me take any decision regarding him? He failed his matriculation exams because of sheer irresponsibility. All I did was to give vent to my displeasure. And you ? You didn't eat for eight days.

PADMA. Oh, please don't rake up all the failures of the dead boy. You could never stand him, really. Your only son.

BHAU. And what did you do for him? I've never said it before. But there are limits to my capacity for patience. All you did was protect him whenever he did anything wrong. What else did you do for him? Now three times a day you go and tidy up that Raja's room, you wash his clothes. You sit by him when he eats. And Shashi? When he came home on holiday after a whole year, you couldn't be bothered to cook. So you gave him only plain bread.

PADMA. So you mean . . . that I . . . I killed my son!

BHAU. That's not what I'm trying to say. He's gone. His time was up and we were not destined to enjoy a son's love. But our grief isn't going to be any the less by blaming each other for what happened.

PADMA. Must I live alone then for the rest of my life?

BHAU. Why alone? I'm with you.

PADMA. You're not with me.

BHAU. What haven't I done for you till now?

PADMA. How many more times are you going to throw that question in my face?

BHAU. You're twisting things again.

PADMA. You want me to be overwhelmed by gratitude for the rest of my life, don't you? But I am. Have I ever denied all the things you've done for me? If that's not enough, I'll have every article in this house marked as a gift from you to me.

BHAU. Why do you behave as if I'm in the wrong?

PADMA. I do not. I'm actually admitting all my mistakes. What more do you want of me?

BHAU. Do you want a divorce?

PADMA. What?

BHAU. The way you carry on . . .

PADMA. Do you want a divorce?

BHAU. I've never said I did.

PADMA. Then why did you ask that question? How could you think of it?

BHAU. I was asking if you did. You don't seem to be happy here . . .

PADMA. Look here. Don't you put words in my mouth.

BHAU. With a young, impressionable girl about the house, it's not fair to be at loggerheads all the time. I'm thoroughly fed up, I can tell you that.

PADMA. Then say so. Accept it. Why blame me? I'll go away. You and your daughter can then live here in peace. (*Pause. Then, pleading*) I've lost everything. Don't you understand that?

BHAU. I do, Padma.

PADMA. Then why don't you indulge me a little? It's so long since we sat together talking. Are you awfully put off by me because I look like this?

BHAU. No.

PADMA. What's going to become of me ?

BHAU. You'll be all right soon, Padma.

PADMA. I'm never going to have a place in your life, am I?

BHAU. Don't talk like a fool, Padma.

PADMA. Why do you come home late every day from the club? I wait up for you every night in my room.

BHAU. I had no idea. It's always dark in your room, so I assume you're asleep.

PADMA. I sit in the dark, waiting for you. But it doesn't touch you, does it?

BHAU. We have separate rooms because you wanted it that way, Padma.

PADMA. So?

BHAU. And . . . you know . . . it's a little awkward . . . it's so many days since . . .

PADMA. It used to bore you in the old days too.

BHAU. I used to feel guilty. I couldn't get rid of the thought that I was forcing myself on you.

PADMA. I never complained.

BHAU. Why do you make me say things I don't want to, Padma? Sometimes you'd fall asleep in Leelu's room. Other times you'd take such a long time getting ready for bed. You may think I didn't notice, but I did when you went for your baths in the middle of the night.

PADMA. Why rake all that up?

BHAU. I don't want to. (*Pause.*)

PADMA. I want another child.

BHAU. Padma.

PADMA (*beside herself*). I do, I do.

> *She looks pleadingly at him. Bhau touches here awkwardly. Slowly pulls her*
> *towards him. Both try desperately to overcome their revulsion and come together*
> *in love. A vain attempt. Finally, Padma moves away repulsed.*

BHAU. Now who doesn't want whom? Forget it. Padma, get rid of all these silly
ideas. You should know that you can't have another child now.

> *Padma springs up. Catches hold of Bhau's shirt and shakes him violently.*

PADMA. What did you say? Say it again. Say it. (*Gradually calms down.*) Let's go.
Let's go out there. I can't bear to be in this room. (*They enter the drawing*
room and come face to face with Leelu. Padma, shouting). What were you
doing here? (*Leelu begins to go in.*) Leelu. (*Leelu stops in her tracks.*) You
were eavesdropping, weren't you?

BHAU. Padma.

PADMA. Weren't you?

BHAU. Padma, let her go.

PADMA. You don't know her and her tricks. She's becoming too smart for her
age. You were listening on the sly, weren't you? And what were you doing
in Raja's room?

LEELU (*smouldering with fury*). At least I wasn't there in a gold-embroidered silk
saree.

PADMA. Say that again.

LEELU (*screaming*). I will. I'll say it a thousand times. I'm ashamed of you. You
are no mother. You're a dirty woman. Look at those letters. These . . .
These . . . all these letters. I found them in your room. (*Throws them down.*)

Dirty, dirty woman, that's what you are. I don't sneak into that Raja's room. It's you that go in there. You go there a thousand times a day.

Bhau slaps Leelu. Leelu is stunned. This is the first time he has raised his hand to her. She recovers gradually and, within a moment, has become an adult. Cut off from everybody, left alone. Calmly, she begins to walk away.

BHAU (*upset, pleading*). Leelu . . .

Leelu continues to walk away without looking back.

PADMA. Don't be angry, please. These letters, they're not even real. Look. Take a look. All of them. Look, they're not even addressed to anybody. They weren't written with anybody in mind. They were just something to do. Something to keep me busy. I used to get so bored. Look at them . . . Please, just look at the letters. (*Stumbles towards Bhau, holding and opening the letters out to him. Bhau stands still, looking at her with profound pity.*) Why don't you look at them? At these letters? I . . . I'm not what you think I am. I'm not. (*Pleading*) I'm not like that. (*Suddenly beginning to sob.*) Forgive me, please. I have no one. Please don't leave me.

Bhau caresses her hair.

Curtain.

PARTY

TRANSLATED BY ASHISH RAJADHYAKSHA

The play in its original Marathi version was first performed by Aniket on 26 August 1976 at the Chhabildas Hall, Bombay, with the following cast:

DOCTOR	Anant Bhave
DAMAYANTI	Rekha Kamat
SONA	Neera Adarkar
BARVE	Madhu Bhatt
AGASHE	Bal Karve
BHARAT	Dilip Kulkarni
VRINDA	Chitra Palekar
JAGDAND	Pramod Phalke
MOHINI	Suneela Pradhan
MALAVIKA	Madhuri Sardesai
NARENDRA	Amol Palekar
LIGHTS	Bal Moghe
STAGE	Nalen Bhivandkar
	Sham Karandikar
PRODUCFION CONTROL	Vijay Shirke
PRODUCTION DESIGNED AND DIRECTED BY	Amol Palekar

Party was made into a film in Hindi in 1984 by Govind Nihalani, with the playwright contributing the screenplay and fresh dialogues. While Nihalani himself wielded the camera, Nitish Roy was the art director, and Renu Saluja the editor. Produced by the National Film Development Corporation of India, it featured Rohini Hattangadi, Manohar Singh, Vijaya Mehta, Deepa Sahi,

M. K. Raina, Soni Razdan, Shafi Inamdar, Akash Khurana, Gulan Kripalani, Amrish Puri, Om Puri, Naseeruddin Shah and Pearl Padamsee. It was in colour, and had a running time of 155 minutes.

A veranda to the left of stage, in front. Further behind, on a slightly raised platform, Sona's bedroom. A living room to the right. A large swing on the veranda. A single bed and a cradle. As the curtain opens, only the room is lit. Damayanti, aged 45, a little tense, evidently used to luxury but now self-consciously sober in her living habits. The Doctor, also 45, simple, a homely sort, with an ordinary face that is nevertheless perceptive and intelligent.

DAMAYANTI. Is it after seven?

DOCTOR. No.

DAMAYANTI. It's dark outside.

DOCTOR. It's only half past six.

DAMAYANTI. I'm cold.

DOCTOR. We're almost into winter.

DAMAYANTI. Would you pass me my wrap . . . over there? Thank you.

DOCTOR. Aren't you well?

DAMAYANTI. Of course I am.

DOCTOR. I could give you a tablet or something.

DAMAYANTI. We shouldn't have had this party tonight.

DOCTOR. Too late to say that.

DAMAYANTI. These parties get on my nerves.

DOCTOR. But you don't stop throwing them every week.

DAMAYANTI. One has to do these things.

DOCTOR. Then face it.

DAMAYANTI. I wonder if Bhattacharya got his invitation. Hard to get through to him. If he's shooting somewhere, he'll have to drop out.

DOCTOR. Bharat must've told him.

DAMAYANTI. I hope so.

DOCTOR. Why don't you relax now?

DAMAYANTI. You know I can't. Not until this is over. Thanks, anyway.

DOCTOR. What for?

DAMAYANTI. For coming over early.

DOCTOR. I know your jitters when you throw a party.

DAMAYANTI (*teasing*). And so you come early. I swear I wouldn't last even one if it weren't for you.

DOCTOR. Nonsense. (*Pause.*)

DAMAYANTI. I wish I could do that.

DOCTOR. Do what?

DAMAYANTI. Manage a party by myself. But there are always so many things to do. And I'm terrible at making conversation. And all those awkward moments.

DOCTOR. I'm not much help there for I speak the least.

DAMAYANTI. But you look after everyone. You supply the drinks. You get the cigarettes . . . You notice little things so I can relax. (*Pause.*) Thanks for the roses.

DOCTOR. Welcome.

DAMAYANTI (*teasing again*). So considerate! Isn't he thoughtful! And understanding !

DOCTOR (*quietly*). Thank you.

DAMAYANTI. Do you feel I depend too much on you?

DOCTOR. No.

DAMAYANTI. Do you depend on me? (*Teasingly*) Don't say no. I'll be mortified.

DOCTOR. I wasn't going to say yes.

DAMAYANTI. Playing the romantic again?

DOCTOR. That's a new line? Am I?

DAMAYANTI. Then am I? (*Suddenly turns serious, more to change the tenor of conversation.*) I don't play—I am a romantic. (*Laughs.*) We're talking rubbish.

DOCTOR. Are we?

DAMAYANTI. I suppose we're all romantic, I mean to some extent. But we're tempered with realism too. Unlike Amrit.

DOCTOR. Is he a romantic?

DAMAYANTI. Isn't he? He had this strange idea of living with those tribals . . . Gonds, aren't they?

DOCTOR. Yes.

DAMAYANTI. What's he going to *do* there? Ruin his health. He's scrawny enough to begin with.

DOCTOR. You're mixing idealism up with romanticism.

DAMAYANTI. How? The two go together.

DOCTOR. Actually Amrit isn't even an idealist. He's convinced that many people in our society are exploited and there's nobody on their side to fight for them. So he's gone across—that's all. As simple and straightforward as that, the way he sees it.

DAMAYANTI. I'd forgotten you had a soft corner for him. He should have been here now. So many things happening. Did you see the documentary Bhattacharya made on Natarajan's paintings? Amrit would've loved it. He was always on to some project or other of his own. He wanted to write and direct an opera once.

DOCTOR. Who are we to decide his priorities for him?

DAMAYANTI. He's a fool. Natarajan plans to settle down in Vienna. Amrit's versatile enough to have done what he liked. We need men like him in our theatre, in our films.

DOCTOR. What's the use of discussing all this?

DAMAYANTI (*uneasily.*) Why isn't anyone coming?

DOCTOR. They won't come before seven.

DAMAYANTI. They were supposed to come here directly after the felicitation.

DOCTOR. Whose turn today?

DAMAYANTI. The Young Writers Association. A formal programme.

DOCTOR. Does he really enjoy it?

DAMAYANTI. Who?

DOCTOR. Barve.

DAMAYANTI. He can't help it. But Barve has a strange weakness. He can't refuse anyone. I keep telling him how he wastes half his time because he can't say no.

DOCTOR. Forget the time. Think of the embarrassment he goes through.

DAMAYANTI. Through what?

DOCTOR. In all this . . . living in the limelight. All those garlands and speeches and photographs.

DAMAYANTI. Oh, one gets used to all that.

DOCTOR. The very idea gives me the shivers. (*Pause.*) Aren't you changing your saree?

DAMAYANTI. Should I?

DOCTOR. You decide. I merely mentioned it.

DAMAYANTI. It's all right. Isn't it?

DOCTOR. It's too informal. Aren't you having this party in Barve's honour?

DAMAYANTI. It's going to be informal. He wouldn't like a speech.

DOCTOR. I wonder.

DAMAYANTI. You're prejudiced.

DOCTOR. I'd forgotten how much he meant to you.

DAMAYANTI. Don't be sarcastic now.

DOCTOR. Sorry. I didn't mean it that way. (*Pause.*)

DAMAYANTI. Don't you think he deserves it?

DOCTOR. What?

DAMAYANTI. This award.

DOCTOR. Who am I to decide . . .

DAMAYANTI. Don't evade!

DOCTOR. With all these eminent people expressing their opinions, how does mine matter? In fact, I don't have an opinion about it. I don't understand art. You know that. And if an award is only a measure of popularity, I'm sorry I haven't anything to say to that either.

DAMAYANTI. He deserves the award.

DOCTOR. Did I say he doesn't?

DAMAYANTI. He deserves it. (*Pause.*) I'm not judging his greatness or his creative achievement. But it is the first time a Marathi writer has got this award. And in Marathi at least, he's the best we have.

DOCTOR. Your regional sentiments are to be applauded.

DAMAYANTI. And he is my friend.

DOCTOR. That's reason enough, then.

DAMAYANTI. Don't you think he's magnificent?

DOCTOR. I hardly know him.

DAMAYANTI. He's donated the entire award money to a lepers' colony. And he runs so many trusts. He keeps saying it's the duty of the well-to-do to help those less fortunate. He has a sense of moral *obligation*.(*Pause.*) And why are you so quiet?

DOCTOR (*amused*). I was wondering if I could've done all that.

DAMAYANTI (*gushing*). I'm sure. You're the one perfect man I know.

DOCTOR (*more amused*). Thank you.

DAMAYANTI. Should I really change? This one's pretty shabby.

DOCTOR. Don't go by what I said. I don't understand these things.

DAMAYANTI. I wouldn't believe that. They loved the saree you bought me in Banaras.

DOCTOR. Bit of luck, your liking it.

DAMAYANTI. I wanted to wear it tonight.

DOCTOR. You can, still.

DAMAYANTI. It doesn't matter. I don't feel up to it.

DOCTOR. Sona? (*Damayanti nods.*) Is she still the same?

DAMAYANTI. She refuses to come out of it.

DOCTOR. It was a cruel blow.

DAMAYANTI. But for how long is this to go on?

DOCTOR. You must be patient.

DAMAYANTI. I'm worried about Sona. (*Pause.*) Why don't you have a word with her?

DOCTOR. We've spoken already, once.

DAMAYANTI. She's being really strange. She refuses to speak to me. And when she does, I think it's only to hurt me. I go to pieces listening to her.

DOCTOR. I'll speak to her again.

DAMAYANTI. You may get across. She only gets along with you and Amrit of our friends.

DOCTOR. Amrit would've been the right man. He's of her generation . . .

DAMAYANTI. She hates people coming here. And now she's worse than ever. I was responsible for her meeting Sahani.

DOCTOR. What about the baby?

DAMAYANTI. It's healthy enough.

DOCTOR. Does Sona look after it well?

DAMAYANTI. She does because she feels responsible. I haven't seen her play with the baby. (*Pause.*) Why should this have happened to her?

DOCTOR. Don't get neurotic. It won't help.

DAMAYANTI. She doesn't want me within her sight. As though I'm somehow responsible.

DOCTOR. Damayanti . . .

DAMAYANTI (*angry*). She hates me.

DOCTOR. Please now.

DAMAYANTI (*now uncontrollable*). I'll go round the bend one day. I'll need you then, very much. (*Pause.*) I saw him yesterday.

DOCTOR. Sahani?

DAMAYANTI. Yes. He'd come to the Centre for the rehearsal. I couldn't help myself, I asked him why he'd done this to my daughter.

DOCTOR. Why did you speak to him?

DAMAYANTI. He's a villain. He puffed at his pipe and said he was ready to marry her. But Sona didn't want to. (*Pause.*) I sometimes feel Sona shouldn't have done that.

DOCTOR. Do you think she would have been happy?

DAMAYANTI. He might have come round, finally.

DOCTOR. He's a playboy, you know that.

DAMAYANTI. Does that mean she should be so vicious to us? We're going to have people over now. I've no idea how she'll behave tonight.

DOCTOR. You must help her through.

DAMAYANTI. Oh, yes, I do that, don't I? She makes me feel guilty. She's become so . . . so ascetic that even our normal life seems like an indulgence. And this party . . . This isn't indulgence. One has one's obligations. (*Sona enters from the bedroom. About 25, a tight, plain face, without any make-up, and tense, her eyes burning harshly.*) Are you ready?

SONA. Do you want to order beer?

DAMAYANTI. It's all right. They drink whisky.

SONA. I won't come out.

DAMAYANTI. What do you mean?

SONA. They're your friends.

DAMAYANTI. But they want to meet you.

SONA (*bitterly*). I know.

DAMAYANTI. It wouldn't look nice. Barve's fond of you, you know.

SONA. What do you expect me to do?

DAMAYANTI. Sona! Really!

SONA. I've made the arrangements. The cook's been told what to do.

DOCTOR. Sona, change your saree, my dear.

SONA. Please, uncle!

DOCTOR. Listen. I'll be just as bored tonight. I'd like you to be with me. (*Pause.*)

SONA. OK.

DAMAYANTI. Look, I haven't changed my saree either.

SONA. To show off! To show how worried you are about me. (*She leaves.*)

DAMAYANTI (*hurt*). I didn't mean that.

DOCTOR. Now, Damayanti!

DAMAYANTI. Why does she behave like that with me? (*Pause.*) I haven't told you yet . . . Agashe has proposed . . . I mean, he's still interested.

DOCTOR. In what?

DAMAYANTI. In Sona. You know . . . he wants to marry her.

DOCTOR. I should have guessed as much.

DAMAYANTI. It's just like Agashe, isn't it?

DOCTOR. Now don't mention this to her. She'll only get more violent. What a vulgar man, that Agashe. Coming out with this kind of proposal when she's barely out of her trauma . . .

DAMAYANTI. He probably means well.

DOCTOR. Must you deceive yourself?

DAMAYANTI. He's spoken to Sona already.

DOCTOR. Did she tell you?

DAMAYANTI. No, Agashe told me.

DOCTOR. And then?

DAMAYANTI. She refused. (*Pause.*) I asked Sona to spend a few days with my father in Delhi. He does love her. And she's the only grandchild of an only daughter.

DOCTOR. She'd only have got more upset there. Does your father have time for life outside of diplomacy?

DAMAYANTI. What do you think of Agashe? He's coming tonight.

DOCTOR. My evening's ruined.

DAMAYANTI. He's not that bad.

DOCTOR. Oh, he's friendly enough. I can't speak to him for more than a minute. He's always about his cars and air-conditioners.

DAMAYANTI. He's a good sort.

DOCTOR. His damned smugness and sickly charm . . .

DAMAYANTI. He'd have got offended. I've always invited him. At least, he's always got himself invited. And Barve's coming tonight, so . . .

DOCTOR. Yes! And Agashe's a successful writer too.

DAMAYANTI. What are you hinting at?

DOCTOR. Nothing.

DAMAYANTI. Do you think I'm stupid enough to be impressed by these people's glamour?

DOCTOR. We've known each other for twenty-five years.

DAMAYANTI. You're being unjust. Agashe needs me. If Papa weren't a Cabinet minister, and I didn't have a bit of influence, he wouldn't have even noticed me on the street.

DOCTOR. Agashe needs everybody. To make something of his cars and air-conditioners.

DAMAYANTI. You're getting too serious. And unnecessarily. Agashe's a climber. He has a bit of talent as well, even though he's in the commercial theatre.

DOCTOR. Talent? Or success?

DAMAYANTI. Bharat isn't a success, but I've invited him.

DOCTOR. What's got into you lately?

DAMAYANTI. What?

DOCTOR. Why do you go on like this?

DAMAYANTI. Bharat's a good boy.

DOCTOR. I marvel at your ability to confuse issues. Are we discussing his goodness or his writing?

DAMAYANTI. He's nice. A bit awkward, and overly ambitious at times. But he's risen from the lowest strata. So that would happen, I suppose.

DOCTOR. Your bunch will dismember him.

DAMAYANTI. You're being not only unjust but also positively vicious.

DOCTOR. You know I'm right. I'm only a ringside spectator watching your glittering world. . .

DAMAYANTI. A nice position to be in.

DOCTOR. And highly amusing.

DAMAYANTI. Must we be fighting?

DOCTOR. Are we?

DAMAYANTI. You're demoralizing me. You haven't a nice thing to say about any of my *friends.(Pause.)* You're prejudiced against all creative people.

DOCTOR. A discovery! Why?

DAMAYANTI. Because you aren't creative.

DOCTOR. That's damned funny.

DAMAYANTI. Say anything you like, but look after Agashe tonight.

DOCTOR. What kind of revenge is this?

DAMAYANTI. He might annoy poor Sona.

DOCTOR. Don't get me close to Agashe. I'll concede everything to you.

DAMAYANTI. I didn't mean that. You can stick to your mouldy opinions. Nobody cares about them anyway. But Agashe *can* be a nuisance. If not Sona, he'll get after Mohini.

DOCTOR. Mohini's old enough to look after herself.

DAMAYANTI. She hasn't been herself lately. I told Barve so. But he's so caught up with himself . . .

DOCTOR. I think she wants to get married.

DAMAYANTI. I don't think so. She's lived with Barve for seven years. They would have got married by now if they'd wanted to.

A light falls and spreads on the veranda. The living room dims, and outside we see Barve, Mohini and Bharat enter. Barve—45, thoughtful, self-absorbed, intelligent. Mohini—30, unusually beautiful, but with a hurt look and a petulant manner. Bharat—24, skinny, sensitive, self-conscious and awkward.

BHARAT. Your purse . . .?

MOHINI. Eh?

BHARAT. Your purse!

MOHINI. So?

BHARAT. You've forgotten it in the car. Shall I fetch it?

MOHINI. Don't bother.

BHARAT. It wouldn't be a bother. (*He rushes out.*)

MOHINI. Let's get home early tonight.

BARVE. All right.

MOHINI. You don't mind.

BARVE. Not at all.

MOHINI. Do you feel like being here longer?

BARVE. It doesn't matter.

MOHINI. Don't drink too much now.

BARVE. OK.

MOHINI. And let me be by your side all the time.

Damayanti at the door of the living room and veranda.

BARVE. Not late, are we?

DAMAYANTI. Oh no. We've all the time. And you're the first.

BARVE. I hope it isn't a very big affair.

DAMAYANTI. It's informal. I thought we'd relax a bit tonight. (*As they speak, they enter the living room.*) Agashe's coming. And Vrinda. She's got a bone to pick with you, by the way. She called up a while ago.

BARVE. Probably wants to know why I didn't give the money to the Communist Party.

DAMAYANTI. Put on your shawl.

BARVE. Let it be.

DAMAYANTI. It's cold.

BARVE. Let it be, I said.

Bharat enters.

BHARAT (*to Damayanti*). Hullo!

DAMAYANTI (*a little patronizingly*). Come in, sit down. (*To Barve*) How was the programme?

BARVE. They're always the same. They exhaust you. I thought you'd be there. Eh, Doctor?

DOCTOR. Too many cases today.

MOHINI. You do look tired!

DAMAYANTI. Would you like to lie down a bit?

BARVE. Oh, she's always imagining things.

DAMAYANTI. Where did Bharat catch up with you?

BHARAT (*injured*). I didn't.

MOHINI. He was at the programme. We offered him a lift.

BHARAT (*trying to joke*). So you caught up with me.

BARVE (*ignoring him*). Where's Sona?

DAMAYANTI. She's dressing. She'll be down.

BARVE. Where are my cigarettes?

MOHINI (*guiltily*). I forgot them.

BARVE. Tch . . .

DAMAYANTI. He'll fetch some. (*To Bharat*) Won't you? Come on, kid, have some respect for your seniors. You have to do all this.

BHARAT (*angry within*). I'm not a kid.

DOCTOR. Your brand's Capstan. I have some.

BARVE. Thanks.

DAMAYANTI. Bharat's angry, Barve.

BARVE. Good.

BHARAT (*embarrassed*). Nonsense.

DAMAYANTI. We enjoy watching you get angry.

BHARAT. Why should you enjoy seeing anyone angry?

DAMAYANTI. You're our local angry young man, aren't you?

BARVE. Desperado!

MOHINI (*to Barve*). May I have a puff?

BARVE. Have a *cigarette*. (*Passes her the pack.*)

MOHINI. No-o-o, just a puff.

BHARAT. You can tease me if you like. I wasn't angry.

DAMAYANTI. Go on, get angry, we don't mind you. It's because you're angry that you're a good writer.

BHARAT. You praise me only in private.

DAMAYANTI. You want me to say this in public?

BHARAT. Why not?

DAMAYANTI. Nobody listens to me. Do they, Barve? Tell me if they do. I'll buy a loud-hailer tomorrow.

BHARAT. You don't have to go on like this.

DAMAYANTI. You can't be in a hurry for recognition. You must wait your turn. Do you know how much Barve had to struggle?

BARVE. It needn't always be like that. Not everyone has to struggle as much as I did.

BHARAT. I don't mind struggling. And I don't care for recognition. (*Pause.*) I turned down the state-government award, in case you didn't know.

DAMAYANTI (*suspicious, but laughs uncertainly*). Are you teasing Barve?

BARVE. No, he isn't.

BHARAT (*imploringly, to Barve*). I didn't mean anything like that.

BARVE. I know. Our positions are different. I respect yours.

BHARAT (*continuing imploringly*). Please don't misunderstand me.

BARVE. It's all right.

MOHINI. Darling . . .

BARVE. You . . .

MOHINI. May I sit beside you?

BARVE. This party's for Mohini, isn't it?

DAMAYANTI. Yes. But she'd never come without you, so it's for you too.

MOHINI. You haven't visited us for ages, you haven't.

BARVE. When did we invite them?

MOHINI. We plan to, soon. (*Embarrassed laughter.*)

DAMAYANTI. Once Mohini bolts the door from within, she forgets the rest of the world. And then it's just Barve and herself. Right?

MOHINI (*imploringly*). No . . . Yesss!

DAMAYANTI. Forget it. We weren't cadging invitations. We're hardly strangers.

BARVE. Sona still hasn't come down.

DAMAYANTI. I'll fetch her.

BARVE. Let her be. She'll come.

DAMAYANTI. I was wondering whether you could talk to her, Barve!

BARVE. If it's going to help.

DOCTOR. No, Damayanti

DAMAYANTI. Let him. She likes Barve.

DOCTOR. Leave her alone. You'll only make it worse.

BARVE. It's an unfortunate business.

DAMAYANTI. What's the way out, Barve? (*Pause.*)

BHARAT (*doubtfully*). Perhaps she should keep herself busy.

> *Pause. Bharat is ignored, and withdraws, a little offended.*

BARVE. It's easy to say that.

DAMAYANTI. I told her to take up her research work again. She was fanatic about that only a year ago. But nothing seems to interest her now. It's become quite a problem.

MOHINI (*unsteadily*). May I see the baby?

BARVE (*a trifle sharply*). No, Mohini.

DAMAYANTI. Let her. It may help Sona out of her mood. (*Pause.*) She may recover sooner if she knows we're still by her side.

> *Sona, at the door adjoining the bedroom and living room.*

BARVE. Hello, Sona.

SONA (*dry*). Hullo.

BHARAT (*uncertain*). Hullo.

MOHINI. Come, sit here.

SONA. Do you want the drinks now?

DAMAYANTI. You sit. I'll fetch them. (*She goes inside.*)

> *A heavy silence for a few seconds.*

BARVE. Are you on to your research again?

SONA. Yes.

BARVE. That's good.

SONA. Why? (*Pause.*)

Damayanti enters with the glasses and drinks.

DAMAYANTI. Where' s Agashe, I wonder?

Agashe at the door. Aged 40, with a paunchy, prosperous look.

AGASHE. Enter the devil.

DAMAYANTI. Where's Vrinda? Why isn't she with you?

AGASHE. I'd called her. She doesn't travel in capitalist cars, you know.

BHARAT. You're no capitalist.

AGASHE. She thinks I am. Anyone who earns comes under the label.

BHARAT. Do you mean you're rich?

AGASHE (*shrugging his shoulders, with some flamboyance*). Can't help it, I suppose.

DAMAYANTI. You'd be rich too, if your plays were done commercially.

BHARAT (*proudly*). I couldn't prostitute myself to public taste!

AGASHE snickers). Ha! That one again.

MOHINI. Darling, I don't want so much.

BARVE. Leave it.

MOHINI. Shall I put it in your glass?

AGASHE (*to Barve*). Congratulations, by the way. My heartiest . . . Hullo Sona. Hullo Doctor. See my new air-conditioner some day? Our living room's like the sea breeze these days.

DOCTOR. Ask Damayanti. She knows all about air-conditioners. How did the programme go?

DAMAYANTI. Barve's tired of them now.

AGASHE. It happens. After the two-hundred-and-fifty-first show of my play *Love and Passion*, I'd been through the same mill. One has a responsibility to one's public, I guess. We are victims of public adulation. Can't very well turn them down. I had a dozen shawls before the fever passed. Show them to you some time.

BHARAT. It's hard to say no to people.

DAMAYANTI (*freezing him with a look*). Bharat!

The light grows very dim; only the veranda remains brightly lit. Narendra, Malavika and Vrinda enter. Narendra, 30, sluggish, goodlooking once but now consumed by the good life. Malavika, 20, 'cute', with short hair, fashionable, glittering earrings. Vrinda, 35, with dry hair, a sharp face, cotton saree and a cigarette, always looking for victims.

NARENDRA. Let's go *back*, Malavika . . .

MALAVIKA. Shut up. C'mon in.

NARENDRA. Can't gatecrash like that. We aren't invited. And I'm sleepy.

MALAVIKA. It's supposed to be informal. Isn't it? They won't mind. Right?

VRINDA. Come in if you want to. Don't look to me for support.

MALAVIKA. Let's go in. We can always say we met Vrinda on the way and came with her here.

VRINDA. You're getting me involved.

MALAVIKA. Darling, you can survive this little lie for us.

VRINDA. I don't mind. You've promised to drop me home.

MALAVIKA. Oh su . . . u . . . u . . . re! Right, Naren?

NARENDRA. Will we be here long? I'm tired and want to sleep.

MALAVIKA. Do you sleep all the time? You can manage a few hours without sleep tonight.

NARENDRA. It's not proper.

MALAVIKA (*pinching his cheek*). That was cute! We'll say we only dropped in. Then we can stay.

NARENDRA. Even if they don't ask us?

MALAVIKA. They will, darling. Come on now, you know I love parties.

VRINDA. Make up your minds now.

MALAVIKA. Come on, come on. (*Drags Narendra inside. All three in the living-room light.*) Hi ! We came uninvited.

NARENDRA. We've only come to drop Vrinda. We're . . .

MALAVIKA. We're staying a *while*. May we, Mrs Rane?

DAMAYANTI (*coldly formal*). You may as well.

VRINDA (*imitating Malavika's fluffiness*). She badly wants to. She madly wants to. She loves parties.

MALAVIKA. Come on, don't let me down. Hi, Sona, you're cute. Hi, Barve, we called you a couple of times but your phone's always busy. Well, damn it, you're a millionaire now.

DAMAYANTI. Have some whisky.

MOHINI (*holding her glass out*). I want some.

BARVE. You weren't going to have any.

MALAVIKA. Delighted.

DAMAYANTI. Narendra?

Narendra shakes his head.

MALAVIKA. Go on, have some. Don't sit with such a sour face.

AGASHE (*to Vrinda*). Good evening.

VRINDA. *Bad* evening. I didn't know *you'd* be here.

MALAVIKA. Cheers.

SOME OF THE GROUP. Cheers.

AGASHE. You don't travel in capitalist cars, do you?

NARENDRA. Am I a capitalist?

VRINDA. He's at least young, Agashe, and handsome.

MALAVIKA (*delighted*). Watch my husband falter now.

VRINDA. Doctor, where's your Coca Cola?

DOCTOR. I'm all right.

MALAVIKA. It does get awkward when someone isn't drinking.

DOCTOR. You go ahead.

BHARAT. Nothing like booze in the world.

DOCTOR. Because it's fashionable? Or because it gets you high?

BHARAT (*angrily*). What do you mean? Whaddyou mean!

DOCTOR. Speak Marathi, pal. Your English is rotten. And your grammar gets more erotic when you're angry.

BHARAT. At least I'm not a rotten communist.

MALAVIKA. Truce now.

MOHINI (*more drunk*). They're fighting! Are they? Are they?

BARVE. No, Mohini.

MOHINI. I hate fighting. (*Loudly.*) No fighting. (*Laughs.*)

VRINDA. Bharat drinks because Barve drinks. And Bharat dreams of awards too!

BHARAT. Look, I'll . . . I'm not going to . . .

DAMAYANTI. Leave him alone, Vrinda.

BHARAT. Do you believe this woman? Do you believe what she says?

DAMAYANTI. Calm down, kid, I didn't say that.

BHARAT. Then defend me.

VRINDA. Weakling!

BHARAT. Who's a weakling?

MOHINI. No fighting. No fighting.

VRINDA. You are. You want others to defend you.

BHARAT. And you . . .

BARVE. Stop this. (*To Vrinda*) You wanted to fight with me, didn't you?

BHARAT. You're established. She can't take you on.

DAMAYANTI. You'll be established too, one day.

BHARAT. Don't patronize me.

VRINDA (*sour laugh*). He's green with envy.

Bharat almost splutters with rage.

AGASHE. You can be pretty ruthless.

VRINDA (*training her sights on Agashe now*). Agashe, his envy's visible. He's simple, from a small town. (*To Bharat*) Live with Agashe a bit, he'll teach you how one hides jealousy.

AGASHE. Now, Vrinda . . .

VRINDA. Take him under your wing. Best way to throttle the poor guy.

AGASHE. I know you're a communist, and so you will say all this, but I'm not going to . . .

VRINDA. Agashe. (*A fake reasonableness*) What've you been doing all these days? What's your stuff like? I dislike Bharat, but he's at least original.

BHARAT (*a little pacified, but still sour*). Thanks.

VRINDA. Oh, don't mention it. I wasn't flattering you. You're still a village boy, and you still make fake pretences to sophistication. (*Bharat turns red.*)

BARVE. Shoo!

MOHINI. Shoo!

MALAVIKA. Poor thing.

BHARAT. Shut up.

MALAVIKA. It's a party. All this goes with it.

MOHINI. I'm hot. Are you? Are you, Diwakar? Shoooo!

BARVE. No.

MOHINI. I'm hot. Are you, Vrinda?

BARVE. Give me a drink.

DOCTOR. Sure.

MOHINI. Doctor, me too.

DOCTOR. Yes.

MOHINI (*to Barve*). Shall we go to the veranda?

BARVE. You go. (*Mohini leaves with her drink.*)

DAMAYANTI. Why did Mohini go out?

BARVE. She's probably watching the full moon.

AGASHE. She should've still been on the stage.

BARVE. She never did like acting.

AGASHE. That's unfortunate. We've lost a good actress.

BARVE. She wasn't much of an actress.

    Narendra yawns.

MALAVIKA. Yoo hoo.

DAMAYANTI. Why? She was pretty good in Agashe's *Lovelight in Your Eyes*.

VRINDA. It was a phoney role.

DAMAYANTI. Maybe, but she was convincing in it.

VRINDA. It was a dud role.

BARVE. She had to look beautiful. And Mohini did. Fortunately she's under no illusions.

The room slowly darkens. Light on veranda, where Mohini stands alone. Bharat enters.

BHARAT. Hi.

MOHINI (*lost*). Hi.

BHARAT. Bored?

MOHINI. Eh? No.

BHARAT. Full moon.

MOHINI. Uh huh.

BHARAT. Like it?

MOHINI. Eh? Yes.

BHARAT. Penny for your thoughts.

MOHINI. Me? Which? No! (*Makes an effort.*) How's your new play?

BHARAT. Nothing much *yet*. (*Pause.*) I'm going to stop writing. (*Mohini looks lost.*) Nobody likes my writing.

MOHINI (*making another effort*). Don't say that. (*Pause*). Diwakar speaks highly of you.

BHARAT. Diwakar? Oh, Barve? Didn't know what you meant. (*Enthusiastically*) What does he say?

MOHINI. Are they fighting?

BHARAT. Who?

MOHINI. I hate fighting.

BHARAT. What was Barve saying about me?

MOHINI. Barve? Hm. I've forgotten. Said you'd be famous one day.

BHARAT. I admire Barve terrifically.

MOHINI. Give me your drink. (*Pours his into her glass.*)

BHARAT. Why did you leave the stage?

MOHINI. Poor Diwakar. Yeah! For him. Doesn't he need me? I love him.

BHARAT. They were praising you inside just now.

MOHINI. Diwakar? What?

BHARAT. Nothing.

MOHINI. I love him. (*Pause.*) I do love him . . . uh . . . anybody . . .

BHARAT. Eh?

MOHINI. It's painful. (*Pause.*) Glass.

BHARAT. What glass?

MOHINI. Fill-er-up.

BHARAT (*uncertainly*). All right. (*Takes the glass and goes to Barve at the door*)

BARVE. Mohini!

MOHINI. You! Diwakar!

BARVE. What are you doing there?

MOHINI. Come to me.

BARVE. Come inside.

MOHINI. No. Here. Stand here. (*Pause.*) They're fighting.

BARVE. Don't drink any more.

MOHINI. Let's go home.

BARVE. Not now. It'll look bad.

MOHINI. Let it.

BARVE. Are you mad?

MOHINI. Let's go.

BARVE. This party's for us.

MOHINI. For you. Not for me. I don't mind, oh I don't mind. I want you. (*Pause.*) Diwakar. (*Pause.*) Say I'm yours.

BARVE. I'm yours.

MOHINI (*digests his words, then shakes her head, slowly, for a long time.*) Then why does it hurt me so much? Hold me. (*Pause. She goes to him.*) Why am I so restless even when you're here? (*Puts her head on his chest.*) Can't take this, you know, any of this. Let's go home. (*Bharat comes back with Mohini's glass. Seeing them together, he is embarrassed.*)

BHARAT. Your glass. (*Gives it to her and goes back inside.*)

BARVE. Don't take it.

MOHINI. Let me.

BARVE. You're high.

MOHINI. So? You have some. With me. Now. Here, come on. (*Barve has a sip.*) You never share a drink with me nowadays. (*Suddenly, from her daze, comes alive with a shock.*) You never! You always drink alone, you never share a drink with me. You don't share anything!

Damayanti at the door, with a shawl.

BARVE. We're just coming in.

DAMAYANTI. It's all right. I thought you might need this.

Damayanti gives Barve the shawl and goes in.

MOHINI. Did she give you that?

BARVE. It's cold here.

MOHINI. I'd bought you that. Why did you take it from her? Who's she?

BARVE. Mohini!

MOHINI. Who is she? Who is she?

BARVE. Don't drink any more.

MOHINI. Yes. But who is . . . who is she?

BARVE. That's enough.

MOHINI (*again comes alive with a shock*). When I gave you that shawl, you said you didn't want it.

BARVE. Are you going to make a scene, Mohini?

MOHINI. No-o-o . . .

BARVE. Then come inside.

MOHINI. Do I make a scene?

BARVE. Come on.

MOHINI. Do I make a scene? Hold me close. Just this once. For one minute. (*Barve holds her but without emotion.*) Seven years. I loved you. And I've loved you more. And more. And you hurt me. (*Shudders.*)

BARVE. Come inside. You're feeling cold.

MOHINI. I love you.

BARVE. I know. Come on now.

MOHINI. I love you. You say that.

BARVE. I love you.

MOHINI. No, not like that. The way you used to say it. You've changed, Diwakar. You go in. (*Looks at the shawl with eyes full of hatred.*) And throw that shawl away.

BARVE. We'll leave soon. But you don't drink any more. (*He goes inside. She returns to her drink.*)

MOHINI. It's painful. So painful. S . . . o . . . o . . . o . . . o painful. (*Sona enters.*) Sona! It's painful.

SONA. What is?

MOHINI. It hurts.

SONA. What does?

MOHINI. To be in . . . (*Pause, as she remembers.*) . . . love. (*Sona is clearly wounded.*) I'm sorry, dear, sorry.

SONA (*controlling herself*). It's all right.

MOHINI. I'm really sorry. Ve . . . r . . . r . . . r . . . ry sorry.

SONA (*irritated*). I said it's all right.

MOHINI. Do you know? He can't live without me.

SONA. Barve?

MOHINI. Diwakar. (*She wakes up.*) Barve. Yes, Barve. Such fun. Everyone calls him Barve.

SONA. Now stop drinking.

MOHINI. I've stopped everything. For him. Even the s . . . tage. Singing. I was a star.

SONA. I know.

MOHINI. Am I bad? To look at?

SONA (*takes a deep breath*). Bad! You look like the queen of fairies. (*Mohini titters.*) What's the matter?

MOHINI. A fairy? You know white? Laundry?

SONA. Laundry?

MOHINI. Apsara Laundry. Near our house.

SONA. Don't drink now.

MOHINI (*angrily*). Why not? Why NOT? He . . . because he doesn't want my shawl. (*Starts crying.*) I'm bad. I look old.

Damayanti is again at the door.

DAMAYANTI. Mohini! Sona? What's the matter? She's drunk.

SONA. Mohini!

MOHINI. Sorry.

DAMAYANTI. Will you lie down in Sona's room for a while?

MOHINI. No. Don't (*pause*) worry. I'm not drunk.

DAMAYANTI. You lie down.

MOHINI. Did I make a scene?

DAMAYANTI. You didn't.

MOHINI. I did, I did.

DAMAYANTI. Come inside now.

MOHINI. I made a scene.

Damayanti takes Mohini into Sona's room. As Sona watches them go, a little angrily, Agashe comes out.

AGASHE. I thought Mohini and Mrs Rane were here. (*A little uncertain.*) I thought . . .

SONA. They aren't. Can't you see that?

AGASHE. Why are you getting angry?

SONA. You needn't have looked for that excuse to come here.

AGASHE. I really . . .

SONA. That's enough.

AGASHE. Who do you think you are? You aren't the only girl I know.

SONA. Then why add me to your harem?

AGASHE. You are insufferably arrogant.

SONA. I despise your kind.

AGASHE. Stop it now. Wait for five years. When you start getting wrinkles.

SONA. You're despicable.

AGASHE. All right. My offer still stands.

SONA. Offer? Offer?

AGASHE. My proposal.

Sona runs into the living room, passing Vrinda and Bharat who are coming out to the veranda.

VRINDA (*to Agashe*). Now what did you say to her?

AGASHE. Why should I say anything?

VRINDA. You must've proposed to her again.

AGASHE. Nonsense.

VRINDA. Try proposing to me some day.

AGASHE. You don't want my capitalist car, but you don't mind my capitalist self?

VRINDA. One's husband can be a capitalist. My father's a millionaire. One needn't travel in his car.

BHARAT (*trying to make a joke*). One can't choose one's parents.

VRINDA. One can definitely choose one's husband.

AGASHE (*on his way to the living room*). At your age? Ha!

VRINDA. Insect!

Bharat is also leaving.

VRINDA. Bharat! Where are you going?

BHARAT. Inside. I thought . . .

VRINDA. Scared I'd seduce you?

BHARAT. Huh. (*A little nervous.*)

VRINDA. Stay. (*Pause.*) I'm sorry about what I said earlier. I didn't mean all of it.

> *Darkness again. Light on the living room. Damayanti, Barve, Agashe, Narendra, Malavika, Doctor and Sona.*

MALAVIKA. Wake up, Naren.

NARENDRA. Can't help it.

MALAVIKA. Actually I should go with that delegation.

NARENDRA. You? It's for writers.

DOCTOR. You could write on the art of baking a cake.

DAMAYANTI. Nothing's fixed yet. Papa only mentioned it the other day. You know how they drop these ideas around in Delhi. It mayn't even come off.

AGASHE (*to Barve*). You'd go, I suppose.

BARVE. I don't want to go anywhere now. I'm trying to concentrate on my novel.

DAMAYANTI. You can't drop out. You're essential.

BARVE. I've been there, twice.

DOCTOR. Bharat should go. And Amrit.

DAMAYANTI. Nonsense.

DOCTOR. What's wrong?

DAMAYANTI. They're too young.

DOCTOR. That's why they should go.

DAMAYANTI. What's Amrit written? He's been away three years.

BARVE. I've always been uncertain about Amrit's writing. He seems to not have settled into his medium yet.

DAMAYANTI. And Bharat? He's unknown, outside our group.

DOCTOR. So what? How many people have heard of Barve in America? Apologies, Barve. Bharat's young. He has new ideas. He'll grow with experience.

DAMAYANTI. He can't pour tea straight. He's awkward, he fidgets. You need dignity to go abroad.

DOCTOR. I've seen Americans digging their noses.

MALAVIKA. Eeee!

NARENDRA (*startled*). What happened?

MALAVIKA. You're a nose specialist!

DAMAYANTI. Why do you say things like this?

DOCTOR. It's the young who represent us best abroad. They're young and immature but they have a vitality that Barve hasn't. He's too set in life. And he's hardly what you'd call Young India.

DAMAYANTI. You can say all you like about these boys. But Barve's going has obvious advantages. How can you deny that?

BARVE. The Doctor's right, in a way. I'm old now.

DAMAYANTI. Nonsense. You're creatively younger than even Bharat. Bharat has a raw strength.

AGASHE. Say that to him and he'll start wagging his tail.

BARVE. Such language!

AGASHE. Send me.

DAMAYANTI. Who am I to decide?

AGASHE. You?

DAMAYANTI. Really.

AGASHE. So you'd act innocent. But you know that you've only to pass the word to your papa in Delhi for . . .

DAMAYANTI. What do you mean, Agashe? Do you imply that I pull strings? Do you think I'm . . . I'm so disintegrated? Apologize.

DOCTOR. He should apologize to the Marathi theatre.

AGASHE. You're commercial. This delegation's only . . .

AGASHE. What's commercial? Our plays run. People see them. Barve's play may have three hundred shows and get translated into fourteen languages and sell film rights—but he's not commercial.

DAMAYANTI. He's avant garde. That's the word.

DOCTOR. Bharat's avant garde.

MALAVIKA. Eeee! You're spoiling the evening. Send me. Me and Sona. Right?

Sona smiles politely, a little artificially, then gets up and goes to her bedroom. Mohini's sitting there, her head in her hands. Darkness over the living room as the bedroom light goes on.

SONA. How do you feel?

MOHINI. I was sick. I threw up.

SONA. Are you better?

MOHINI. What's the time?

SONA. I haven't a watch.

MOHINI. Your kid's sweet. (*Sona is quiet.*) Sona darling, don't be so angry. Never hate your child.

SONA. Please!

MOHINI. I love children. I had a dream once, with lots of my children around me. I'd comb his hair, put her to sleep as I stitch something for a doll. What's the noise outside?

SONA. They're enjoying themselves.

MOHINI. I hate parties. I do. (*Pause.*) Diwakar gets lost with people. He forgets me. And when he drinks . . . (*Pause.*) I used to hate drinking once, but I drink now. You know, he snores all night and I lie wide awake. Even when I'm drunk, I can't sleep. I only feel dizzy. I want to snuggle deep into his arms but then I get scared he'll wake up and get angry . . . I lie down then, still and wide awake as my head spins with fatigue. (*Pause.*) I'm telling you all this private stuff . . .

SONA. Don't, if it's difficult.

MOHINI. I'm a wreck. My head's splitting.

SONA. Pull yourself together.

MOHINI. So I use make-up. But it's strange. The fashions these young girls flaunt. They look so fresh and blooming. I'd look ten years older if I happened to be with that crowd. I've lost touch with the outside these seven years. I'm so involved with Diwakar.

SONA. Don't bother with fashions. You don't need fashions. They'll never be you with all the fashion in the world. You're you.

MOHINI. I? (*Takes a deep breath.*) I'll lose my looks one day, and that'll be the end.

SONA. Why don't you act again?

MOHINI. It's too late. I'm thirty, you know! (*Pause.*) I had a lovely voice once but it's gone.

SONA. You'll learn again, if you try.

MOHINI. I've been wanting to, for so long. I'm stuck. I want to live. But I keep saying that as long as I know Diwakar loves me, I'd be happy. I need peace to start my career again. It never happens. (*Pause.*) Perhaps I'm too demanding.

SONA. Do you want to go out?

MOHINI. I don't feel up to it. I made a scene just now.

SONA. Of course not, there was nobody there.

MOHINI. Is my hair all right? That purse . . . my lipstick's inside. Do you like this shade?

SONA (*confused*). I don't know.

MOHINI. Does it suit me? Does it go with my saree? (*Disappointed.*) I've lost my sense of taste. I keep thinking I'm badly dressed and people are laughing at me.

SONA. I don't understand these things. I've never used make-up. Plain people only look worse with make-up.

MOHINI. I went to Yasmin the other day, for a facial. And she said, 'Madam, don't you ever use cosmetics. You don't need them.' (*Pause.*) I won't come out.

SONA. Why? Don't do that.

MOHINI. No. I don't understand a thing of what they say. And they'll only be polite.

SONA. Stop thinking about other people.

MOHINI. Get me a drink here.

SONA. Are you sure?

MOHINI. Yes, I'm better now. Only one. To boost my courage.

Sona returns to the living room. Light now on the veranda. Vrinda and Bharat are sitting close to each other, Vrinda, subtle and seductive.

VRINDA. Are you still angry?

BHARAT. I never was.

VRINDA. Don't misunderstand me, Bharat. People will always think me aggressive. But they don't understand me really. Do you promise?

BHARAT. What?

VRINDA. That you'll never misunderstand me again.

BHARAT (*swelling*). I understand human nature. I'm used to seeing things objectively.

VRINDA (*now with an effort*). I know. That's why I'm telling you this. (*Puts her hands out.*) Promise.

BHARAT. Is it necessary?

VRINDA (*not moving her hands*). Come on. Get out of this awkwardness.

BHARAT (*lets her hold his hand*). I promise.

VRINDA. We'd better not. (*Dropping his hand.*) You'll think I'm cheap.

BHARAT. Of course not.

VRINDA. I'd like to tell you something.

BHARAT. You can tell me. We are friends now.

VRINDA. How can you get involved with these people? They are nothing but a bunch of show-offs.

BHARAT. Now that's what I call flattery, Vrinda—Vrinda-tai.

VRINDA. Oh, call me Vrinda. You don't have to be formal with me.

BHARAT (*hiding his pride*). Do you consider me a genuine writer?

VRINDA. You are original. Why don't you understand that?

BHARAT. But Lady Damayanti doesn't think so.

VRINDA. Why do you give so much importance to these people?

---

* Elder sister in Marathi.

BHARAT. It's not a question of importance. I get angry. They can be so blatant. None of them has even suggested my name for the delegation going to the USA.

VRINDA. Want to go to the Soviet Union?

BHARAT (*eagerly*). Of course. Anywhere, really. I want to go abroad.

VRINDA. I'll talk to my Party friends.

BHARAT. Haven't you left the Party?

VRINDA. So what? I have my friends.

BHARAT. I'll be really grateful, Vrinda.

VRINDA. Shall we go together?

BHARAT (*shocked, but holding himself in control*). Lovely idea.

VRINDA. Better not. You'll be saying I'm chasing you.

BHARAT. Nonsense.

VRINDA. Show me your hand.

BHARAT. Do communists like you believe in the future?

VRINDA (*trying to make a joke*). I'm a Disillusioned Communist.

BHARAT. And these are your illusions.

VRINDA. Wise guy. I know you. Show me your hand. (*Grabs his hand.*)

BHARAT (*embarrassed*). I haven't trimmed my nails.

VRINDA. We'll manage. You're not part of that bunch of pseudo-sophisticates, anyway.

BHARAT (*with exaggerated vehemence*). I don't even wish to be one of them.

VRINDA. I wouldn't want to hurt you, but I should tell you something: Beware of these people. They'll strangle you, this clique.

BHARAT. All of them? Agashe'd like to, but Barve?

VRINDA. You are a simpleton. Barve? They're all into this. Professional jealousy, it's called. No writer, however great, is free from it. They'll dangle you around the edge of their glamour world, and then it'll be too late for anything. I've seen this happen even in our Party. (*Pause.*) Your hand's hard. Don't ever let it get like theirs if you really want to survive.

BHARAT. Did these people treat Amrit like this too?

VRINDA. Sure.

BHARAT. That's why he went away, then. He was frustrated. They say he was disappointed in love. (*Pause.*) Whatever happens, I'll never quit the battlefield like that.

VRINDA. Forget Amrit. I could never understand that man. You're the one with a future now. (*Squeezes his hand.*)

BHARAT. Now tell me the truth.

VRINDA. I mean it. I'm not reading your fortune. I've seen your work and I can tell.

BHARAT. That I'm a good writer?

VRINDA. One of the best we have.

BHARAT. Sometimes I really lose my confidence. I keep thinking people find me ridiculous.

VRINDA. Forget people. And forget popularity.

BHARAT. But I write to be popular.

VRINDA. Awww. Rubbish.

BHARAT. Really! I need recognition. It would make me feel more secure. What am I now? But if I'm famous, I'll at least feel assured of my existence. You think all this is fashionable, existential talk, right? It's true. I need other people to see myself like I need mirrors. People who tell me I exist.

VRINDA. If it's popularity you're after, then you'll have to write like Agashe.

BHARAT. No. No. I could never write such plays. Because, basically, I'm honest. I do want recognition, but only by remaining honest to my personal experiences and without making any compromise. But recognition I do want. (*Pause.*) The more I think, I wonder if it isn't just a clever excuse I've cooked up.

VRINDA. Your analysis is brilliant. And that is the greatest quality of your writing. But what holds you back . . . I can't understand one thing. I don't want to underestimate or reduce your work, but . . .

BHARAT. About my writing?

VRINDA. Yes.

BHARAT. What can't you understand?

VRINDA. Forget it. You'll think I'm shameless.

BHARAT. Go on, please.

VRINDA. Why do you have such adolescent ideas about sex? They're bookish and romantic and hidebound, unlike the white-hot passion in the rest of your work. How old are you, by the way?

BHARAT. Twenty-four.

VRINDA. It's time you experienced life as an adult. You're too inhibited. Aren't you?

BHARAT (*scornfully*). Huh!

VRINDA. Get married.

BHARAT. Just now?

VRINDA. The best time. But marry a rich and well-connected girl. It helps.

BHARAT. How?

VRINDA. You could travel, see places. You could concentrate on your writing. Shall I help you find someone?

BHARAT. No, no.

VRINDA (*taking his hand again*). Show me. I'll tell you what sort of a wife you'll draw.

BHARAT. Rich. And ugly.

VRINDA. Not ugly. But, well, not beautiful. And definitely rich. And clever. She'll help shape your career for you.

Malavika and Narendra enter.

MALAVIKA. Palmistry classes? Tell me.

VRINDA. How could you desert poor Barve?

NARENDRA (*yawning*). Oh god! (*Another yawn.*)

MALAVIKA. I thought there'd be some music and a bit of fun. This one's been a bore.

VRINDA (*to Bharat*). Do you dance?

BHARAT. Nawww.

MALAVIKA (*to Narendra*). Let's dance!

NARENDRA. Without music?

MALAVIKA. Yup, without music.

They dance closely together, Narendra yawning and with his eyes shut.

VRINDA (*to Bharat*). Let's dance.

BHARAT (*uncomfortably*). I don't know how to.

VRINDA. I'll show you.

BHARAT. Really, I can't.

VRINDA. It's easy. You have to learn a lot of things now.

Bharat stands up awkwardly, they dance a little stilted piece. Malavika stops.

MALAVIKA. Tch. It's no fun.

Narendra leans against a pillar.

MALAVIKA. Aayyyy!

NARENDRA. Eh? Let's go home?

MALAVIKA. Oh, wait. (*She goes in, Narendra follows her.*)

BHARAT. That's enough.

VRINDA. One-two-three. One-two-three. That's it.

BHARAT. They've gone in.

VRINDA. One-two-three, one-two-three. (*She holds Bharat tight. A little dazed, a little scared, he dances stiffly as Vrinda's arm behind him grips his body. She draws her face close to his. He draws away and runs into the living room. Vrinda, abashed and a little scared*) Bharat! Come back, I was only joking. (*Sona comes into the veranda from the bedroom.*) He's dumb. I was teaching him some steps and he just . . . panicked. How're you?

SONA. All right.

VRINDA. I didn't speak to you inside. Thought you'd only feel more awkward. (*Pause.*) I passed on your message to Sahani.

SONA. Thanks.

VRINDA. I hope you don't think I'm responsible.

SONA. How are you involved?

VRINDA. I'd warned you. When you were getting too friendly. He's a cad. I told him yesterday he could do what he liked with your letters. You wouldn't see him. I got him a little shocked there.

SONA. Do me one more favour, Vrinda. (*Pause.*) Tell Agashe something.

VRINDA. What?

Pause.

SONA. Tell him to keep out of my way. (*Pause.*) He wants to marry me.

VRINDA. I see!

SONA. He pesters me all the time. He keeps staring at me. I can't bear to be in the same room with him.

VRINDA. If you don't mind, what's wrong?

SONA. Vrinda!

VRINDA. He isn't that bad. Not too intelligent but . . .

SONA. How could you! After all that's happened. I hate them. All these men.

VRINDA. You're getting too melodramatic. (*Pause.*) Did you tell your mother all this?

SONA. She wants me to marry him too. Let's change the subject.

VRINDA. You'll think I'm unscrupulous. But Agashe's a good catch. Look at your condition. And he's asking for you.

SONA. He's vulgar. And so are you.

VRINDA. Go on, I don't mind. One can't stay unmarried for too long. It isn't easy.

SONA. For you?

VRINDA (*casually*). I don't mind, I have all this Party work anyway . . .

Damayanti *appears at the door.*

DAMAYANTI. Come inside, both of you. What's going on here?

VRINDA. We're trying to avoid Agashe.

DAMAYANTI. Stop it. What did you do to Bharat?

VRINDA. Me?

DAMAYANTI. He's sitting and sulking in a corner. He looked scared when he came in.

VRINDA. Oh that! I was only teasing him because he couldn't dance.

DAMAYANTI. Now come in. Barve's missing you. (*They go in. In the veranda now comes Jogdand—25, lean, intelligent, plainly dressed. He has a sharp gaze and quick movements. Voices from inside. Lights come on in the drawing room. He comes to the door and Damayanti sees him.*) Jogdand! What a surprise!

DOCTOR. Jogdand.

DAMAYANTI. Didn't you go to Dharagad to meet Amrit?

JOGDAND. Returned this morning.

VRINDA. Hi, reporter!

JOGDAND. Journalist. Investigative.

DOCTOR. How's Amrit?

JOGDAND. He's all right, I suppose. I didn't know you had a party here tonight.

DAMAYANTI. What's the news?

VRINDA. Some bad news definitely. Jogdand doesn't get along with good news.

JOGDAND. That's true.

DAMAYANTI. Go on then.

JOGDAND. Amrit's been arrested.

An uneasy silence.

AGASHE. That's all? I thought it'd be worse.

DAMAYANTI. This is unexpected.

DOCTOR. I thought things had quietened down there.

DAMAYANTI. What do you mean?

VRINDA. Don't you people read the papers? Amrit's organized the adivasis over there. There are demonstrations there every day.

DAMAYANTI. When did this come out? I read only the reviews.

MALAVIKA. Came in small type, probably.

DOCTOR. It's an uncertain peace out there. Things flare up overnight, or at least people can make things flare up.

MALAVIKA. Why does Amrit get involved in all this violence? An artist like him!

JOGDAND. I didn't say Amrit does.

MALAVIKA. Who, then?

JOGDAND. Do I have to spell it out?

DAMAYANTI. The police would have to be present at a demonstration . . .

JOGDAND. Do you think the police are there to maintain peace?

AGASHE. You're on Amrit's side.

JOGDAND. I don't take sides. I'm a journalist, I record facts. You can see them for yourselves. Take a look there some day. An experience of a lifetime.

MALAVIKA. I saw some tribal dances one day . . . They were fantastic.

BARVE. How did all this start?

JOGDAND. You seem to know nothing about it.

BARVE. I've been in Delhi this last month.

JOGDAND. Precious little news gets published anyway. But I'm going to publish the whole story . . .

DAMAYANTI. What's happening?

JOGDAND. The armed police have been posted there for the last fifteen days. On adivasi lands. Amrit's been taking out demonstrations of hundreds. A stone hurled from somewhere hits a policeman. Then there's a lathi charge. Then teargas shells. A show of rifles. Very dramatic. Very, very dramatic.

VRINDA. Very stupid. Peaceful demonstrations don't bring about revolutions.

JOGDAND. He doesn't claim to be bringing about revolutions.

VRINDA. It isn't one. It won't lead anywhere. We argued about this before he left. Social work may be a good thing in itself but you can't mistake it for revolution.

JOGDAND. Theories don't concern me just now. Nor, in fact, Amrit. He wants to work. I want news.

BHARAT. What's the government doing?

JOGDAND. It's doing enough. It's giving adivasi land to industry. It's deforesting the entire area. It's giving licences and facilities to a couple of big promoters. Facilities like water, which adivasis had to walk two miles to get.

BARVE. There must be some development plan being implemented.

JOGDAND. Indeed. That plan caused a furore at the Vidhan Sabha.* They wanted that very land although it's inaccessible. Because once that forest area is developed, land prices around it will shoot up. And who do you think owns all that land? Our beloved chief minister's wife. They're spending crores of state funds to build a canal now.

BARVE. How can this be?

JOGDAND. Charmed by your innocence, to be sure.

DAMAYANTI. Jogdand!

MALAVIKA. They must be very poor, these adivasis.

VRINDA (*contemptuous*). They can't afford cars, so they hunt on scooters.

---

* Legislative Assembly, the lower house of state legislature in the different states of India.

DAMAYANTI. Isn't the government going to compensate the tribals?

JOGDAND. Fifty rupees for a new hut, and fifteen days' rations. In fifteen days they move out, or get thrown out.

AGASHE. And if they don't agree? Fifty rupees should be worth something to them.

JOGDAND. You should ask them what they feel about it.

VRINDA. Did Amrit speak to you?

JOGDAND. He'd have liked you to have been there, and seen all these people. But they'll take at least fifty years to build an airstrip there.

VRINDA. What else?

JOGDAND. That's all. He doesn't speak much anyway. But you should see him with the tribals.

DAMAYANTI. He had a lovely laugh. A little ray of sunshine. There was a time when he'd write frequently to Sona, wonderful little incidents about the life there.

VRINDA. What do the adivasis think of him?

JOGDAND. I'd gone to do a story for my paper. But now I feel like writing a book. (*Pause.*) You wouldn't believe the atrocities. Some people burnt down their huts one night when I was there. Three children and a woman were killed, and when Amrit took the injured fifteen miles away to a doctor, the clinic was shut. Or had been deliberately shut. They tried to bribe Amrit, and then began threatening him. He's alone there—fighting.

BHARAT. We're always alone in our battles.

JOGDAND. Our little battles in the air.

BHARAT. Everyone's struggle is different. Because we all see our lives differently. We attain self-realization through different means.

JOGDAND. Lord!

AGASHE. I think I'll make a trip there one day.

VRINDA (*peevishly*). Don't go. You might get caught! Go later when there's no firing.

AGASHE. It's a great theme for a play.

MALAVIKA. Rich versus poor. Surefire.

BHARAT. The poor are the innocent, loving, suffering people, the rich the bad, murderous guys. A sacrificial, widowed sister, a truant but well-meaning brother, a postman who unravels the meaning of life with phrases like 'the stamp of emotion on the envelope of life, the postcard of love falling into the dead letterbox of existence'. And a wise station master singing, in Technicolor, of how the train of life waits but briefly on the platform of happiness . . .

DAMAYANTI. Stop making fun of the poor man, Bharat.

BHARAT (*pleased with himself*). A hymn at the beginning, a lullaby of revolution at the end. The actress playing the adivasi girl putting on coloured clothes and a flower in her hair.

JOGDAND (*sighing*). That's better. I needed a bit of this to recover from Amrit's lofty heights.

VRINDA. Bharat thinks he's funny.

BHARAT. Can it. I'm just previewing some of Agashe's forthcoming spices.

JOGDAND. I wasn't talking about Agashe.

DAMAYANTI. Have a drink.

JOGDAND. Thanks, I need one.

Mohini comes out, a glass in her hand.

DAMAYANTI. How do you feel?

MOHINI. Give me a drink.

DAMAYANTI. Are you better now?

MOHINI. Just a drop. O . . . n . . . n . . . n . . . ly a drop.

NARENDRA (*uncontrollably sleepy*). Is anyone in that bedroom? I want to sleep.

MALAVIKA. Shut up, have some . . .

NARENDRA. Damn it, let's go home.

AGASHE. That's Sona's room.

SONA (*with animosity*). What do you mean by that?

AGASHE. Men are forbidden there, lest they desecrate it. Isn't that so?

SONA (*getting up*). You . . . I hate you. (*Goes into her bedroom.*)

DAMAYANTI (*shaken*). Agashe . . .

AGASHE. Why did she have to do that?

DAMAYANTI. That remark was most uncalled for. We're all trying to help her.

AGASHE. Sorry. (*For him, that's the end of the matter.*)

DAMAYANTI (*as she goes in*). That was really unfair. I hope she isn't . . .

    Darkness over the living room as the bedroom area lights up.

SONA (*in a fevered rage*). Throw that dirty lot out.

DAMAYANTI. Darling . . .

SONA. And you too—get out of the room.

DAMAYANTI. Sona!

SONA. Leave me alone. Please.

DAMAYANTI. Steady, Sona.

SONA. Or let me go from here.

DAMAYANTI. Keep your temper, Sona. You'll only make things worse. (*Pause.*) And you must be able to take it by now.

SONA. Why should I?

DAMAYANTI. It isn't your fault. But we can't help what other people say. (*Pause.*) Agashe spoke like a fool. But he must have been provoked. Did you say something to him earlier? I don't like you to behave in public like this.

SONA. Why did you insist on my coming out then? I didn't want to . . .

DAMAYANTI (*suddenly tired*). It exhausts me too. I haven't the strength to keep up with these tensions any more.

SONA. Tell Agashe not to get in my way again.

Pause.

DAMAYANTI. Agashe asked me today . . .

SONA. You know my answer.

DAMAYANTI. What's wrong with Agashe?

SONA. Mother!

DAMAYANTI. He doesn't love you. But nor did Sahani.

SONA. I loved Sahani—and I don't even like Agashe.

DAMAYANTI. Sahani was a cheat.

SONA. So's Agashe. He only wants our money. And your contacts.

DAMAYANTI. Most marriages happen like this. And most succeed. (*Pause.*) Why do you think your father married me?

SONA. You told me he loved you.

DAMAYANTI. I thought so too, then. He wasn't my kind of man. I realized it too late. But I didn't walk out on him. Papa was a leading lawyer and a national politician. He saw the uses of that.

SONA. Papa's dead. He can't tell his own story.

DAMAYANTI. Sona, it was awful. There wasn't a night when he didn't get drunk.

SONA. Why did he drink? Did you ever wonder?

DAMAYANTI. The question haunted me. Fact was, he didn't lack anything. I saw to that. I introduced him to cultured people, to the finer things of life. But he never cared. He only lived for the flesh.

SONA. You nagged him.

DAMAYANTI. Sona . . .

SONA. Yes, you did.

DAMAYANTI. That's unjust.

SONA. And I've always hated you for that.

DAMAYANTI. God!

SONA. If Papa were alive today, he'd have behaved differently. He'd have said: Sona, shoot Agashe. Shoot all of them.

DAMAYANTI. And would that have solved the problem?

SONA (*bursting out*). What is it? What's this problem of mine that's eating you? I'm ready to live with dignity with my child. And you think it a problem!

DAMAYANTI. I wouldn't be able to behave in the irresponsible manner your father did.

SONA. You made him miserable and now you want to make me miserable. You were ashamed of Papa and you are ashamed of me. I have no looks, I don't have the delicate manners of your friends. I'm not accomplished like they are. You may forget it, but I have not. How many times you've taunted me, saying that, like Papa, I live on the surface. And why? All because I do not sit with this medley of pseudo-artists around me. Our lives are healthier for that. And if you must talk of flesh, I'm not in the least ashamed to say that I live in the flesh.

Long pause.

DAMAYANTI. Where is this going to get you?

SONA. You're responsible.

DAMAYANTI. Punish me, then. I'm exhausted.

SONA. Papa was like a lion. He was wonderful. But he was simple. You gave him a complex, with your so-called intellectual behaviour.

DAMAYANTI. That's not true. I shared my friends, my choices. But I never imposed anything on him. Nor on you.

SONA. True. You simply ignored me. You tucked me away in a boarding school in Simla the moment Papa was gone.

DAMAYANTI. Sona darling, it was the best school in . . . (*Demoralized.*) It's useless.

SONA. And kindly keep all your boyfriends away from me.

DAMAYANTI (*angry*). What did you say?

SONA. You can lick the glamour off their hide. Leave me out of that.

DAMAYANTI. I'm not going to take this from you.

SONA. You're a parasite. You feed on other people's glamour, and you think it's yours. You wanted Papa's money. And you want these people's glamour. You've got both. Clever, aren't you? You've got both.

DAMAYANTI (*roughly*). I haven't touched a rupee.

SONA. I know that image of yours. But you did have it all in the bank where—

Damayanti slaps Sona. Then, shocked, she goes over to her and sits.

DAMAYANTI. I'm sorry, Sona.

Sona glares at her. Then runs to the living room. Darkness over the living room. Light on the veranda. Vrinda and Agashe.

VRINDA. Don't think I'm chasing you.

AGASHE. Wouldn't be a novel experience.

VRINDA. Oh, sure, you're the glamour boy of the theatre, aren't you?

AGASHE. Bharat wouldn't like that. He'd be jealous.

VRINDA. He's a stupid, immature child.

AGASHE. He was flirting with you a while ago.

VRINDA. By the way, the cat's out of the bag now.

AGASHE. Indeed?

VRINDA. You've revealed yourself.

AGASHE. What are you going to charge me with tonight?

VRINDA. I knew you were a fake writer. But I wouldn't have believed anyone telling me you were such a fake—until tonight.

AGASHE. But what's your basis for such a dim view of me?

VRINDA. It's a good theme. The rescue of a poor unwed mother. Write a play. Everyone who can't stand such people in real life will come and cry their eyes out in sympathy. Five hundred shows at least!

AGASHE. I see.

VRINDA. Make the heroine simple and gullible. One of those helpless, flickering waifs. Because if you make your heroine stupid and aggressive like Sona, your play won't run a day.

AGASHE. So she spoke to you.

VRINDA. She didn't. I got it out of her. You know I love scandals. (*Pause.*) Wind up now, old man. See how many birds you could bag. One, rescue of poor unwed mother, guaranteed tearjerker. Two, Sona's millions. Three, Damayanti's minister-father's political contacts . . .

AGASHE. You enjoy being vulgar, don't you?

VRINDA. Then deny it.

AGASHE (*looking at her steadily*). What's wrong, even if this is true?

VRINDA. Did I say that? So help me, Sona thinks it's wrong.

AGASHE. She'll change her mind.

VRINDA. Yes? And you'll wait for her?

AGASHE. What else can I do?

VRINDA. There's better fish in the ocean.

Both understand each other. They stare at each other till Bharat enters.

BHARAT. Let's dance.

VRINDA. What's eating you, kid?

BHARAT. But just now you . . .

VRINDA (*bluntly*). There's no music.

BHARAT. You were teaching me a while ago.

VRINDA. Don't talk to me like that. Besides, you're in the way.

BHARAT (*insulted*). Sorry.

VRINDA (*to Agashe*). Let's go in.

They go inside.

BHARAT. Pig! (*He looks at them go, and then sits on the swing.*)

Narendra comes out.

NARENDRA (*startled*). Damn.

BHARAT. What happened?

NARENDRA. I thought I'd be alone at least here.

BHARAT. Come and sit. There's place for two.

NARENDRA. Do you insist on sitting there?

BHARAT. I'm here already.

NARENDRA. I thought you wanted to go to sleep.

BHARAT. Me?

NARENDRA. I want to sleep, dammit. Do you mind?

BHARAT. Why should I?

NARENDRA. Then get up. I want to sleep here.

BHARAT. Why don't you go inside and sleep?

NARENDRA. She won't let me. Malavika. Never marry a socialite. (*Slightly on edge.*) Are you getting up?

Bharat gets up and moves towards the living room. Narendra quickly stretches out. By the time Bharat turns to look at him, he's fast asleep. Light on the bedroom. Damayanti sitting, lost. Barve comes to the door.

BARVE. We're leaving.

DAMAYANTI. So soon?

BARVE. Mohini isn't feeling well. And you're sitting here alone.

DAMAYANTI. I was about to come out.

BARVE. Don't. Jogdand and Agashe are having a violent argument.

DAMAYANTI. Is that the noise?

BARVE. We must leave. Mohini's high.

DAMAYANTI. Is it true then?

BARVE. That Mohini's becoming a heavy drinker?

DAMAYANTI. Yes. (*Pause.*) I don't know what's wrong with her.

BARVE. I've stopped thinking about it.

DAMAYANTI. Things seem to be falling apart everywhere.

BARVE. You aren't looking too well.

DAMAYANTI. I'm sick of everything. Sick of this business of living.

BARVE. How can you say that?

DAMAYANTI. Every little thing upsets me these days.

BARVE. You look worn out.

DAMAYANTI. Do I? I never was really beautiful. And now age is catching up. (*Pause.*) We're of the same age. But I've aged faster. What else could happen to a woman like me? (*Pause.*) Do you feel old?

BARVE. I don't know. Not really. I never think about it.

DAMAYANTI. You'll never grow old. You live every moment with zest.

BARVE. What should that mean?

DAMAYANTI. Life has been kind to you. You can devote your energy to whatever you wish to. (*Pause.*) You're at the top, Barve. (*A tired effort at a joke.*) How's the air up there?

BARVE (*seriously*). There is no air.

DAMAYANTI. How do you feel?

BARVE. Lonely.

DAMAYANTI. This feel of power in your better understanding of things, don't you feel good about it?

BARVE. Used to. Used to feel good about the power I had till I reached the top. But now I wonder if the journey's over. And it can be frightening.

DAMAYANTI. But you've achieved something. You may not have received as much as you've given to life, but life hasn't left you empty-handed, you've received something.

BARVE. I'm not sure.

DAMAYANTI. What about me? Look at me. If I die, there's nothing to show that I ever existed. I haven't done a thing to leave a mark.

BARVE. Don't say that. So many people love you. You're one of the most cultivated women I've ever come across.

DAMAYANTI. That makes it only more painful, you know. I can understand someone else's work, accept it, even enjoy it. But it only makes me all the more aware of my own barrenness. You won't understand that perhaps. You'd have to be a woman to understand.

BARVE. Would you be happy if you'd created something?

DAMAYANTI. I don't know. But in my mind, in my blood, what I feel and go through, may be I could have exorcized that. Whenever I see, hear or read something new, I feel, but of course I knew it. It was within me . . . and yet beyond me to express it. And that can be awfully frustrating. (*Pause.*) Barve, you're a happy man.

BARVE. No.

DAMAYANTI. Not materially, but you do have a sense of fulfilment.

BARVE. No.

DAMAYANTI. How can you not?

BARVE. I don't. (*Pause.*)

DAMAYANTI. Why does this happen? To all of us?

BARVE. You know the answer.

DAMAYANTI. No, I don't.

BARVE. You know it. And so do I. But we evade it. We haven't the strength to face up to it. (*Pause.*) We are people who are always running far away from life.

DAMAYANTI. How can you say that? I've made every decision in life because I've believed in something. I've looked after a useless male for twenty years without complaining. I've survived it all because I thought there was something to survive for. Then why is it all in ruins around me?

BARVE. What do you lack?

DAMAYANTI. Barve! You ask me this? You? Because I have a house, a car, some standing and a lot of money? That's all true. But these things have never touched my mind. Few people understand this. Sona's father never could. He wanted me with him at all the parties and functions, decked to the eyebrows in diamonds, talking silly, shallow crap and cheering everyone up. He thought me and my interests ridiculous. In his company, my mind died a slow death, bit by bit.

BARVE. And you let him? Why didn't you struggle to . . .

DAMAYANTI. You may be a genius, Barve, but . . .

BARVE (*with unexpected violence*). I'm not.

DAMAYANTI. You wouldn't understand a woman. Why she lives, and dies, within herself.

BARVE. You should have got a divorce.

DAMAYANTI. That defeat I couldn't have survived.

BARVE. Where's the defeat?

DAMAYANTI. No woman will admit a mistake in love.

BARVE. You are, now.

DAMAYANTI. Only to you. (*Pause.*) Because you understand. Me. (*Pause.*) Why did you donate that award money?

BARVE. To display my generosity, possibly?

DAMAYANTI. Not true. You know that. The conviction, when you announced it . . .

BARVE. That can be faked, Damayanti.

DAMAYANTI. No! No! There was something to it. Something that troubled you. Are you restless?

BARVE (*after a moment*). Yes.

DAMAYANTI. You make me envious. There's something at least happening in your mind.

BARVE. That's not always an advantage.

DAMAYANTI. I feel funny these days. I wake up at nights and can't sleep. Then I stare into the dark. At empty, blind alleys that loom up everywhere. Empty windows, lights with nobody there. I can't bear it. I want to shout, to scream. I regain my breath only when a truck rumbles by or a window lights up.

BARVE. You're used to having people around you.

DAMAYANTI. Oh, no. I do not want any people. I made a scene the other day. Aimlessly, I had wandered about the whole day. Parks, shops, the museum, the library. Then in the middle of the street I stopped. For a moment I didn't know what was happening. Then the tears simply welled up in my throat, to my eyes. I couldn't hold them back, and then . . . in the middle of the street, I broke down. In the middle, and all those people stood staring at me. I wept and wept. Barve, what has happened to me? Why does this happen? Like that, I mean. There is a stillness within me. It's so quiet there. Nothing moves. Not a leaf on a tree. But the eyes well up. The tears flow incessantly. Barve, I need someone. I need you . . .

BARVE. If there's anything I can do . . .

DAMAYANTI. I don't know.

BARVE. Don't hesitate to ask. I shall be happy to do it for you.

DAMAYANTI. You can't do anything, probably . . . no one can.

Damayanti breaks down and sobs. Barve strokes her bent head. The Doctor comes in for a moment and then leaves.

BARVE. Get up.

DAMAYANTI (*wiping her eyes, back in control*). I'm sorry.

BARVE. The Doctor looked in.

DAMAYANTI. He doesn't really understand. He's patient enough, and a real help. Especially with this business of Sona's . . .

BARVE. What does he feel about it?

DAMAYANTI. About what?

BARVE. About my donating the award money.

DAMAYANTI. He appreciates it.

BARVE. You don't have to be polite.

DAMAYANTI. He does.

BARVE. He's uncanny. It's like he can read people's minds. He observes everything, without saying a word, without reacting. It can be quite annoying.

DAMAYANTI. Why do you react so strongly?

BARVE. In a sense, I respect him. He is the only one among us without any ambition.

DAMAYANTI. He cannot have any. In a sense he lives on a flat key. But what ambitions do you have, anyway?

BARVE. Well, not to go down from where I am. And not to let anyone reach where I am.

DAMAYANTI. What's wrong with you today?

BARVE. Don't worry about me. I'm seldom so truthful about myself.

DAMAYANTI. This is not being truthful. It's just self-laceration.

BARVE. We use all these beautiful and deceptive words. The greater the mean-ness, the more beautiful and more deceptive the words. (*Pause*.) I should know. I've been in this business all these days, covering up lies with beautiful words.

DAMAYANTI. Why do you say this? What about the truth you've discovered about life?

BARVE. Have I discovered it? And do I have the courage to face it were it to come and stand before me suddenly and recklessly? No, Damayanti, for the last twenty years I have gone on creating the illusion of having dis-covered the truth. (*Pause*.) When I was going to Delhi to receive the award, the train suddenly stopped in the middle of a jungle. And there, as now, it was revealed to me. It was raining hard. I looked out and saw a few poor women and children standing there, shivering in the rain, looking with indifference at the train. And then it dawned on me. I, all that I wrote, my cultural fund, my contribution, my standing—they meant nothing to them. Or to millions like them. So then what meaning has art? Or, for that matter, civilization? Have they the right to claim to stand by the suffering of these people? I could see no relation between my words and the agony of the endless suffering of these people. My words are no words. They are like an outer skin that can be discarded. (*Pause*.) Amrit knew this. That is what made me feel uncomfortable in his presence. (*Pause*.) Maybe Amrit had realized this when he went away.

DAMAYANTI. He went because he'd written himself out.

BARVE. How do you know? Because we didn't accept what he wrote? Maybe he'll write better yet, after this.

DAMAYANTI. Maybe. Imagination itself can be the source of experience.

BARVE. That's another self-deception practised for long by cowardly artists.

DAMAYANTI. How about Shakespeare? And Vyas?* Shakespeare didn't have to live Hamlet's dilemma himself.

BARVE. Shakespeare was a genius. I am not. And that makes all the difference.

DAMAYANTI. You're exasperating.

BARVE. I'm being honest. And only to you. I've been careful not to reveal this in public. I am a good writer, and clever too. I have been on my little pinnacle for twenty years, haven't I? I set trends. I'm able to keep that bit ahead of most people. I position myself as someone who understands life, so I can feed people with bits that they take to be the real thing. I'm a little better at this than Agashe is. I'm not so stupid. I speak of real events at least. But they're not the truth. This pinnacle's going to collapse like an anthill before too long. A hundred years? I'd be lucky to survive ten.

Pause.

DAMAYANTI. Why are you telling me all this?

BARVE. Because you've been a part of this game. And because Mohini'd never understand.

DAMAYANTI. She loves you.

BARVE. That's the problem. That's why she won't understand. She's so sunk in it that she has eyes for nothing else.

DAMAYANTI. You should look after her.

BARVE. I try. But how can I, eventually?

DAMAYANTI. Why's she turned so touchy?

BARVE. She's guessed, probably.

Pause.

---

* Also known as Vyasa, a central and revered figure in Hindu traditions. He is generally considered the author of the Mahabharata and the scribe of both the Vedas and Puranas.

DAMAYANTI. Guessed what?

BARVE. I don't love her any more.

DAMAYANTI. Oh!

BARVE. You look startled.

DAMAYANTI. I'm not.

BARVE. It is painful. But it happens. The sooner she knows, the better. For her.

DAMAYANTI. She's left practically everything for you, Barve. Her career . . .

BARVE. . . . which wasn't worth a penny. You know she wasn't even a tolerably good actress. She knows it too, subconsciously. She'd never take the risk of returning. She's made her love for me the excuse, and now she can blame me for that.

DAMAYANTI. You're bitter.

BARVE. I'm being coldly analytical. She can't be. She doesn't want to, and she hasn't the sense to understand this for herself.

DAMAYANTI. She's simple, and she trusts you.

BARVE. I know that. And that's why I can't bring myself to tell her all this frankly. Maybe if we lived apart for a while, she'd see it for herself.

DAMAYANTI. I can't see how. For that will leave her adrift in a mindless sea with nothing to anchor her to reality.

BARVE. She's deliberately blinded herself to all this. She's made up her mind not to see anything with her eyes open. She simply refuses to accept reality. And she's started deceiving herself all the more. Any little chore for me, she insists on doing it herself. She can't bear to let the servants even touch my clothes. And she drinks. When I sit down to write, she lies awake in bed and stares at me, unblinking, all night. How many times I've pretended to be asleep, hoping she won't touch me or start crying.

DAMAYANTI. Why don't you speak to her about this?

BARVE. I hate getting involved in one of her scenes. And she won't listen to reason. I feel like going on that delegation abroad, only to get away from her for a few days.

DAMAYANTI. She'd want to come.

BARVE. We could manage that. Tell her there's no foreign exchange or something.

DAMAYANTI. Should I call Papa then?

BARVE. I think so.

DAMAYANTI. I'll do that tonight. (*Pause.*) Bharat's pretty keen to go too.

BARVE. Will you send him?

DAMAYANTI. Maybe I should.

BARVE. I didn't mention this earlier. Thought I'd do it in private. Don't send him anywhere yet. He's gifted. But these cultural exchange rackets could finish him. He needs more time to build himself, to get a little more self-confidence.

DAMAYANTI. He feels we've ignored his latest play.

BARVE. We didn't. We know that.

DAMAYANTI. I didn't mention him in my essay on young Marathi writers in the *Young Artists Journal*. But he's only just begun.

BARVE. Let him feel hurt. Frustrations and struggle are essential to creativity. I don't tell him this because he'd misunderstand.

Mohini at the door, clinging, barely able to stand.

MOHINI. I can sing, like a bird!

BARVE. She's drunk.

MOHINI. Sing like a bird!

BARVE. Let's go home.

MOHINI (*hurt*). Home! There's nothing there. Let me sing . . . I can sing . . . sing
. . . sing . . .

She stumbles, and Barve holds her. Light on the living room.

JOODAND. There's a word for it. Self-deception.

BHARAT. Everyone's destined to do one's thing. Isn't it honest to go by that?

JOODAND. Since when have you started believing in destiny?

BHARAT. I don't believe in destiny. But one does not have the freedom to choose.

VRINDA. You're being awfully inconsistent. Earlier you said you wrote for fame.
Wasn't that your choice?

BHARAT. I was joking. One writes because one has to. You do your social work
because you have to. One must realize this. One must be loyal to one's
work. That is what's important.

JOGDAND. That's an argument used for too long to cover up cowardice.

VRINDA. Well, in Marathi literature, originality means intelligent plagiarism.

BHARAT. Is there any field in which we don't plagiarize? Even in political
philosophy.

MALAVIKA. That was a good one.

VRINDA. Bharat borrows the form even for his plays from other countries. All
the while boasting that his roots are here, that he writes about this soil.

BHARAT. An art form is no country's monopoly. I'll use it if I find it useful. And
Vrinda, you better not dabble in it. You don't understand art or how
content struggles to find its form.

VRINDA. Are we expected to clap?

BHARAT (*trembling*). I know I write crudely. I'm self-conscious and inhibited. I
sometimes strangle my content with my inhibition. Good writing is firm,
yet fragile, transparent—it goes forth like a beam of sunlight as flowers
open before it. Like fragrance to flowers, form should be to content. But

one can see a flower while form is invisible. I'm struggling. Give me time. I know my limitations.

MALAVIKA. What's he saying?

VRINDA. God knows. He's confused.

BHARAT. Oh, yes, I know that. I know that too well.

VRINDA. What are you trying to say?

BHARAT. I? I don't say anything. I show things that relate to what I am, what we all are. What I seek is that tough, burgeoning sprout within the womb of experience. That which remains after the trivia is removed from experience, that which can be articulated. But I can't see it. I must wait. And see what happens.

Barve and Damayanti come out.

BARVE. What's the heat about?

VRINDA. Bharat thinks that he is analysing himself brilliantly.

AGASHE. I don't understand all this stuff. I'm a writer, and I'm diligent about that. With all these problems around us, why do we go and make more for ourselves? Write on the problems of the Dalits. Or on famine, and corrupt ministers. Hundreds of themes lying about if only we'd care to look.

BHARAT. We're reserving them for you. They're your monopoly.

AGASHE. You needn't worry about me. I'm all right. I have four plays performing tonight, all to full houses. And that's an achievement. I'm proud of it. I don't make fake experiments that nobody sees or wants to see. People like my plays not because they're stupid but because something gets across. When I did that *Burning Dreams*. I got hundreds of letters from young women. Because it portrayed their lives. Plays don't become revolutionary only because they're violent or use filthy language.

BHARAT. It's . . . useless.

AGASHE. I get livid with all these avant-garde postures of yours.

BARVE. That's not the question, Agashe. Every writer writes differently because he thinks differently, has different experiences and different problems.

AGASHE. How can one man have every experience? How do I understand other people? By imitating them?

BARVE. That wasn't what I meant. We have to use our imagination. That in itself can be a source for experience . . . (*notices Damayanti*) . . . as Mrs Rane has said. Experience is within us. Critics mock the writer who sits in his room describing the sunset. But we really do understand the sunset best through our imagination. The people we write about are parts of our experiences, parts of ourselves. We bring them to life, making them something else in the way we breathe an autonomous existence into them.

BHARAT. But isn't that part of our personality as well? The shadow of our selves? Or is it a projection into something else?

BARVE. Why not?

BHARAT. I'm not so sure. I don't want to be critical, but in your writing there is so much of yourself that it is no longer something independent. I could recognize your writing from any page of it. You'd call it your own style, but you'd be wrong. Style changes with experience, and with different contents. We should use style only to root the work in the realm of experience—not to break it out of experience.

AGASHE. Bravo!

BHARAT. And if the writer's mind is at all to be revealed in his creation, then at least let it be a great mind. Profound and full of compassion. It forgives all the deformities of life to hold it close to the heart. For it is only in the depths of compassion that all art and religions can bloom.

VRINDA. That sounds like a line from one of Agashe's plays.

JOGDAND. This compassion you talk about, is it confined only to art?

BHARAT. How can it be? It becomes the very being of the person creating it. The artist is, at that moment, all of us.

DAMAYANTI. Bharat's brilliant tonight.

JOGDAND. I don't accept that. When the person fully experiences what he creates, he transcends art and goes into life itself. May be he doesn't create anything. Any art, I mean.

BHARAT. That's impossible.

JOGDAND. Because it's too limited an outlet for change. For that vision of the world which created Buddha or Christ.

BHARAT. Would you call them artists?

JOGDAND. Wouldn't you? In a different, wider sense, in the sense in which religion too stems from art?

DAMAYANTI. You make art didactic. And moral.

BHARAT. And we're trivializing the personal feeling of the artist. Why should every moment of feeling and thought have sociology? We're limiting individual freedom by that.

JOGDAND. This is an interminable debate.

VRINDA. We have to talk these things over. Everyone feels serious then, and full of purpose. Really, Agashe's probably better off than anyone else in not making any claims.

DAMAYANTI. Let it be.

JOGDAND. I must leave. I've to finish my report tonight.

VRINDA. Oh, stay on.

DAMAYANTI. Whisky for anyone? (*Pours some all round.*)

MALAVIKA. To whose health? Or whose what?

BHARAT. To Jogdand!

JOGDAND. No, to Amrit.

ALL. Cheers.

Amid the clatter of glasses, the phone is heard. Damayanti picks it up.

DAMAYANTI. Hello. Who? Yes, hold on. For you, Jogdand.

Jogdand takes the phone, listens for a long time. Nobody pays attention.

JOGDAND (*in a hurry*). I've to rush.

DAMAYANTI. Have some dinner first.

JOGDAND. Please.

DAMAYANTI. What's the emergency?

JOGDAND. Never mind. (*Pause.*) Amrit's been murdered.

Long silence.

MALAVIKA. How tragic! How unfortunate.

MOHINI. What's that? Time to sing? Shall I?

Sings low, off key.

MALAVIKA (*to Mohini*). Darling . . . darling!

BARVE. Keep quiet.

MOHINI. Sorry, Sorry! (*Mumbling*) Sorry!

Silence again.

DAMAYANTI. When did the news come in?

JOGDAND. Officially, only just now. He was released last night. This morning, they found his corpse in a stream in the jungle.

BARVE. Who could have done it?

DAMAYANTI. They're uncivilized, after all.

JOGDAND (*with a touch of anger*). You know, Mrs Rane, the tribals didn't kill him. But they'll be the accused. And the matter will be buried. I am going there. I'll find the truth. (*Bitter.*) And more news for everyone. And the sensation.

Quiet. Sona begins to cry.

DAMAYANTI. Sona! (*Holds her up.*) Be quiet, Sona. It's too much for you to bear, child. Come inside. Now. (She *takes Sona inside.*)

JOGDAND. Doctor!

DOCTOR. Yes?

JOGDAND. Amrit had a message for you. He was grateful to you for the medicine and the money.

DOCTOR (*a little embarrassed*). It wasn't much, really.

BHARAT. Are you going back there?

JOGDAND. I'll have to. Come with me?

BHARAT (*uneasily*). My play begins rehearsals in a couple of days.

JOGDAND. All right. See you. (*Goes to the veranda, followed by Vrinda.*)

VRINDA. Jogdand!

JOGDAND. Yes?

VRINDA. Jogdand!

JOGDAND. Yes, what is it?

VRINDA. No, I won't break down. (*Pause.*) I know I should come with you.

JOGDAND. Will you?

VRINDA. No, I haven't the strength. (*Pause.*) Did he really mention me?

JOGDAND. Yes.

VRINDA. It was too vast a divide for me to overcome. I hadn't the energy. (*Pause.*) We shared the dreams of changing the world together. And then drifted apart. (*Pause.*) See you.

Jogdand hesitates, then leaves. Agashe comes out.

AGASHE. How are you going home?

VRINDA (*taking a decision*). You drop me home.

AGASHE. In my car?

VRINDA. Never mind, come on.

AGASHE. Really, Vrinda? (*He presses her hand. She lets him, not reacting. They go out.*)

Enter Damayanti.

DAMAYANTI. Has Jogdand left?

BARVE. He had to follow up the news.

DAMAYANTI. Vrinda and Agashe have left too.

BARVE. How's Sona?

DAMAYANTI. I've given her a pill. (*Pause.*) What can we do?

BARVE. I don't know. We must help his family. His old mother.

DAMAYANTI. Yes. At least that much.

BARVE. Let's go, Mohini. (*Supporting her.*) Come, Bharat, we'll drop you.

DAMAYANTI. There'll be a condolence meeting tomorrow.

BARVE. We'll see each other there.

DAMAYANTI. Will you speak?

BARVE. I suppose I will. He was a great man, in his own way. Good night. (*Barve, Mohini and Bharat leave.*) Where's Narendra?

DAMAYANTI (*stiffly*). He's asleep. Outside.

MALAVIKA. Look at that. Good night. (*She prods Narendra.*) Yoo hoo, upsy-daisy.

NARENDRA. Eh? (*Startled.*) Are we still here?

MALAVIKA. Uh-huh. Come on, I'll drive. (*As they leave*) Amrit's been murdered.

NARENDRA. Who?

MALAVIKA. Amrit. Don't you remember him?

NARENDRA. Forget it. What's that got to do with us anyway? Let's go. I've to wake up early tomorrow. (*They both leave.*)

The light dims.

REFLECTION

(Pratibimba)

TRANSLATED BY SHANTA GOKHALE

First performed in the original Marathi at Kamatak Sangh Hall, Bombay, on 24 February 1987. Produced by Theatre Unit and directed by Satyadev Dubey with the following cast:

HE	Kishor Kadam
WOMAN	Suneela Pradhan
FLAGS	Ganesh Yadav
GIRL	Rajashri Sawant

First performed in Hindi at Padatik Open-Air Theatre, Calcutta, on 23 February 1987. Produced by Padatik and directed by Satyadev Dubey with the following cast:

HE	Pradeep Roy
WOMAN	Deepti Bhat
FLAGS	Balmukund Hada
GIRL	Isha Uppal

First performance of the second production in Hindi, at Kamatak Sangh Hall, Bombay, on 17 March 1987. Produced by Theatre Unit and directed by Satyadev Dubey, with the following cast:

HE	Naseeruddin Shah
WOMAN	Suhas Joshi
FLAGS	Satyadav Dubey
GIRL	Ratna Pathak-Shah

A pleasant room of the paying-guest kind. It is 7.30 in the morning, but the curtains are still drawn and it is dark. He is fast asleep on the bed. There is silence on the stage for a long time, for so long that the audience should begin to wonder what's happening but without beginning to shuffle and whisper. Suddenly the alarm clock near his pillow goes off shrilly. He doesn't move. The alarm keeps going till it is fully wound down. Again there is silence for a few moments. Suddenly He starts and gets up. For a few moments his movements are quite directionless. Then He stumbles over to the clock, peers at it and says, 'My god.' He puts the clock down in a rush, puts on his slippers and is hurrying to the bathroom when the phone rings. He stumbles back to the clock, realizes his mistake and goes to the phone. As he is about to pick up the receiver, the phone, in sheer malice, stops ringing. Even before he can take his hand off the receiver, the second alarm goes off. While He rushes to the clock, a third bell peals. The doorbell. Confused, He makes for the phone, realizes it's the doorbell and goes to the door. He opens the door and looks out. There's no one there. He shuts the door in disgust and returns to sit on the bed. There is a brief silence. The phone half rings, teasingly. He starts up and looks at it. Then He gathers himself together like an animal waiting to pounce, and stands watching all three—the alarm clock, the phone and the doorbell. But none of them ring any more. Gradually, his tension *disappears. He relaxes on the bed. He is calmer. He gets up, draws open the curtains and throws open the window. Instantly, the thunder of traffic enters the room. He slams the window shut. He picks up his towel and goes to the bathroom. He squeezes toothpaste on to his brush and comes out brushing his teeth. He switches on the radio casually. The radio goes 'ting-tong' and belts out three shrill jingles one after another. The fourth is about to begin when He turns off the radio, utterly disgusted. He continues to brush his teeth, eyeing the audience thoughtfully. He glances at the newspaper. It is blank—there is not a sign of print on it. He reads the paper with great concentration till a meddlesome, coquettish woman of enormous proportions enters through the back door, a cup of tea in one hand and a broom in the other. She bangs down the tea before him. He doesn't even glance up.*

WOMAN. Your tea. (*He is startled.*) How can you sleep for so long, holding up my work and all? (*Starts sweeping the room, continuing to talk without looking at him.*) I get up at four in the morning all ready for the day's work. Who do you think you are? You get up any time you like and expect me to get your tea? Even a paying guest must have some discipline. Is it because I put up with all your nonsense? I'd made it quite clear right at the beginning that I am a woman who believes in doing the right job at the right moment. You were fine the first few days. But now? It's seven, sometimes eight in the morning. And on Sundays—even nine o'clock is too early for you. Is it normal to sleep like this? You should have been named Kumbhakarna. (*She continues to sweep around where He stands, treating his legs like any piece of furniture. He too does not move his legs.*) You're lucky it's me you have to put up with all this, Just wait till you get married. Then you'll be up at five. Not just that. It'll be 'Why do you get up, darling? I'll make your tea. Why don't you stay in bed, sweetheart, I'll fill the water.' I remember all of it. When my husband was alive, I never once had to make the tea or fill the water. He'd even fetch the milk from the centre. It's three years now you've been here. And I've treated you like one of the family. But do you behave that way? Sleeping till all hours as if this were a hotel. (*Gathers the sweeping, straightens up and looks at him for the first time.*) Why don't you say something? Are you angry with me for scolding you? I scold you because you're one of the family. D'you see? DO YOU SEE? (*He opens his mouth to speak and realizes it's full of toothpaste. Pointing to it, He goes to the bathroom.*) I'm glad you brush your teeth before you have your tea. There are people who must have their tea first thing in the morning. Bed tea, they call it. What filthy habits! But you're OK that way. The tea must be stone cold now. Or is that the way you like it? Some people like to pour it into the saucer and blow and blow on and then have it. (*He screams suddenly from the bathroom.*) What happened? (*Pause.*) Did you slip and fall? Shall I come in? Hope you're dressed? Or are you in your underwear? Doesn't wash them for days. Dirty fellow. Only his teeth are worth showing. Can you hear me?

He comes out terrified and stands leaning against the doorjamb. He manages to stumble over to the dressing table where He glances in the mirror and gives a frightened start. He picks up a small mirror from the table and looks at it. and gives another start. Her chatter continues.

WOMAN. Cleanliness is all-important, after all. A person must be clean inside and out, his heart, his clothes, his habits.

HE (*shouts suddenly in a broken voice*). Will you shut up, woman?

For a moment she is dumbfounded. Then she is angry.

WOMAN.What was that you said?

HE. How you go on and on, don't let me think even. (*Drops into a chair.*) Terrible.

WOMAN (*concerned*). What's the matter?

HE. Tell me. Are the mirrors in the house all OK?

WOMAN. What do you mean?

HE. Are they really OK?

WOMAN. What's OK supposed to mean? Don't I wipe them every day? Even mirrors ought to be spotless. It's no use your being clean. If the mirror is dirty, you'll look dirty. Don't you agree?

HE. That's not what I meant. (*Pause.*) Will you come and have a look at the mirror in the bathroom, please?

WOMAN. What for?

HE. Please.

WOMAN. I must know why.

HE. I said, please.

WOMAN. I refuse to enter a man's bathroom.

HE. Please. The mirror.

WOMAN. Oh, all right. What do I do with the mirror?

HE. Tell me what you see there.

WOMAN. You're nuts. What do people see in mirrors?

HE. Look at that one, just once, please.

WOMAN. All right. (*On her way to the bathroom*) Now don't you follow me into the bathroom. (*She goes in. Silence.*)

HE. Are you looking at the mirror?

WOMAN. Yes.

HE. Are you really?

WOMAN. I said yes.

HE. What do you see?

WOMAN. What am I supposed to see?

HE. You can't see anything either.

WOMAN. What do you mean anything? Should I see a ghost? (*She comes out.*)

HE (*impatient, eager*). What did you see in the mirror?

WOMAN. Now you're being childish. What should I see in the mirror? I saw my reflection. That's all.

HE. You did?

WOMAN. Didn't I just? Such a lovely, elegant, graceful jar of ghee.

HE. Did you really see your reflection?

WOMAN. For God's sake. Would I see yours, then? Really! The things you say.

HE. Will you come and have a look in this mirror?

WOMAN. Don't get fresh now.

HE. Please.

WOMAN. There's such a difference in age between us—think of that.

HE. Please, look

WOMAN. I have the purest feeling for you.

HE. Please! Please!

WOMAN. Well. I will if I must. (*Looks at herself lingeringly in the mirror, and is pleased with what she sees. Lost in herself, she begins to hum.*) 'Premnagar mein banaungi ghar mai, karke sab singar!'* This mirror was a wedding gift, you know. It used to be in our bedroom. (*Blushing*) The things we two have seen in this mirror. He was s-o-o-o romantic. Do you think a little girth, just a bit more, would give me just that bit more grace?

HE. Can you see your reflection in that mirror?

---

* 'I'll set up my home in the city of love, bedecked in all my finery.'

WOMAN. Not again. What are mirrors meant for? What do *you* see in them ?

HE. Nothing.

WOMAN. What ?

HE. I can't see a thing in the mirror.

WOMAN. Nothing? Not a thing?

HE. Nothing. I don't see a reflection, nothing. I washed my face and looked in the mirror. Found it blank. Then I thought: Maybe it's dirty. So I cleaned it and looked again. Still nothing. I screamed. Then I thought maybe the mercury's come off. So I took a look at these two mirrors out here. And it was the same, Bai.* I've lost my reflection. It's disappeared. It's gone away. Left me and gone.

WOMAN. Where was the binge last night?

HE. Nowhere.

WOMAN. Of course there was a binge. You're still drunk.

HE. I've not drunk in a week.

WOMAN. Don't lie.

HE. It's the truth.

WOMAN. Come here. (*Walks up to him*) Open your mouth. (*Forces his mouth open and smells it.*) Smells of toothpaste. Are they making toothpaste-flavoured liquor these days?

HE. Stop joking.

WOMAN. It's no joke. You're crazy. How can you lose your reflection? It must be a hallucination. Or your mind is not there. Go and take another look. Get up. I'd like to see how you lose your reflection. Utter rot! You're a

---

* Common word in Marathi used to address women. Often also refers to a female household help.

paying guest here. I'm responsible if you lose something. I don't want to be accused of strange things out of the blue. That's why I'm yelling at you all the time: Take care of your things, lock them up. Don't just sit there. Get up and take a good look in the mirror again. (*He half rises but sits down again, scared.*) What are you scared of? Get up. Go on. (*He shakes his head gloomily.*) What's the use of losing your nerve? Get up. Get up. Come on, up. (*She is all set to hoist him up. He finally gets up, looks at the mirror decisively. A stifled sound escapes him. She hurries across and looks in the mirror with him.*)

WOMAN. Your reflection's really not there. This is the limit. How funny!

HE. You think it's' funny?

WOMAN. We should put it in the papers.

HE (*shouts*). No!

WOMAN. Do you have a recent photograph?

HE. It's not going to be in the papers.

WOMAN. Why not?

HE. No. I won't tell journalists. I won't tell anybody.

WOMAN. Imagine how famous you'll be.

HE. To hell with fame . . .

WOMAN. You'll be world famous in an instant.

HE. Don't want that kind of fame.

WOMAN. That kind and this kind. Fame is fame, after all. Or else, who knows whom in this city of Bombay? Does anyone know anyone else? Eh? Tell me. Does anyone? (*He shakes his head.*) So? Now is your chance. You've been staying with me for the last three years. But I don't know your name. Everyone calls you Blockhead. So I call you Blockhead too. Besides, it's easy to remember. Who'd remember a name? What odd names people have. Blockhead is fine for me. So the point is: as soon as this news appears in the press, people will get to know you. People will throng the doors, windows, both sides of the road, the rooftops and the branches of trees, just to catch a glimpse of you. People will make room for you in buses and local trains, cabbies won't diddle you, clerks, even in government offices, will be polite without provocation. Why! Even if thieves accost you, they'll recognize you and let you go, saying 'What's he got after all?' See? That's fame. Once you're famous, doors will open automatically for you. The whole world will know you as 'The Man without a Reflection'! The wonder of wonders! Travel all over the world. Stand in front of a mirror and hold one-man shows of the Man without a Reflection. Earn lakhs of rupees. Evade all taxes. Stay in five-star hotels. Drink champagne. Get photographed with starlets from Hollywood. But, mind, that's about all. Nothing more. And when you're dead. I'll put up a plaque on this door. 'Here lived the famous Mr Blockhead who didn't have a reflection.' You silly fellow, why do you sit as if you're in mourning? Who's had such luck coming his way?

HE. You won't tell anybody. Will you?

WOMAN. Nobody?

HE. Not a soul. Not the neighbours. Not the family. No friends and associates. No police officers, rationing officers, the RTO men or my boss. They'll cancel my ration card. Take away my driving licence. I'll lose my job.

WOMAN. Do you think all this'll happen?

HE. Yes.

WOMAN. Rot!

HE. Bai, it will.

WOMAN. Nonsense!

HE. People don't care for anything unexpected, unusual or unnatural. They get terrified. And in sheer panic they go on ridiculing the unnatural thing until it drops dead.

WOMAN. Go on. You're imagining things.

HE. I'm telling you. There was this boy in my class at school. He had a lump on his forehead. We teased him, Bumpy, Bumpy, till he threw himself into the pond.

WOMAN. Oh dear! I hope you're not going to kill yourself.

HE. I'd like to.

WOMAN. Not in my house, you won't. I don't mind if you fall ill and die. That's not a suspicious event. But if you kill yourself, I'll never get another paying guest. I'll get a mesh put on that window first thing today. We're on the fifth floor.

HE. Do you think . . . ?

WOMAN. What?

HE. That my reflection doesn't exist because perhaps I don't exist? Can you see me?

WOMAN. What do you mean?

HE. Can you?

WOMAN. Of course.

HE. What do I look like?

WOMAN. For heaven's sake. Like a blockhead.

HE. You mean you can really see me?

WOMAN. I said so once.

HE. You can see my body?

WOMAN. Want me to touch it and see?

She's about to touch him. He squirms.

HE. No, no. Don't. What'll that prove?

WOMAN. Prove? It'll prove you have a body. That it's not lost like your reflection.

HE. How will it prove that?

WOMAN. Now, listen. There are only two ways to prove a body exists. One, by reflection. Two, by another body. One proves the existence of the other. Or else an object has no meaning. Now look at this inkpot. It gets its meaning from this pen. This pack of cigarettes. It has a meaning because of this box of matches. He always used to say, that's my late husband: You are a jar of ghee full to the brim, and me? I'm a beanpole. Like a pretty little mouse sitting on a jar of ghee. That's why we looked so good together. So, you see, if you want to be sure of your body, then you have to depend on another. Now I'm prepared to do anthing that is necessary for my paying guest. It's my job to see that all his needs are taken care of, and that he's comfortable. I take such care of you. I don't even play my LP of the *Geeta Ramayana* or my tapes of the popular writers lest they disturb you.

HE. But bai, is a reflection just a body?

WOMAN. What else? What do you see in the mirror—your mind? Your heart? Your soul?

HE. I wonder. What does a mirror show? What do we see?

WOMAN. Besides, instead of saying we look at the mirror, wouldn't it be more correct to say that it's the reflection in the mirror that looks at us?

HE. That's also true.

WOMAN. There. So your reflection must have got a little bored of looking at you. Thirty years is a long time to be looking at the same thing. It must have got fed up and walked off. How many years of blockheadedness can the poor thing take? Blockheads come a dime a dozen.

HE. Could my own reflection be bored of me?

WOMAN. Why not? Bodies are a tiresome thing anyway. The mind—now that's something you don't tire of. Naturally. Because things are constantly happening in the mind. At least you can make things happen there. You can always think: This or that will happen, or: I'll do this or that. Dream away—colourful, spicy, resplendent dreams. To hell with reflection. You've a mind, don't you? An honest-to-goodness real-and-alive mind? Keep it busy. You won't miss your reflection one bit then.

HE. But now my mind is going to be full of thoughts about my reflection. So it amounts to the same thing.

WOMAN. Why do you go on and on about your reflection? Were you really so fond of it?

HE. Fond of it? I wouldn't know.

WOMAN. So then?

HE. I didn't give it a thought while it was around, though it did scare me a couple of times. That should have put me on my guard. What happened was: there I was, looking in the mirror, looking really hard, you know, asking: Who are you, man? Who are you? Are you the same as I? I kept on asking the question eye-to-eye, with great bravado, keeping my eyes fixed on the eyes in the reflection. And those eyes—they stared back at me, not batting an eyelid. And then those eyes seemed to turn to marbles. If I'd shoved a finger in them, it would have gone straight through and left a dark hole. No blood, nothing. It knocked me right off. I moved away fast. After that, I didn't dare go anywhere near it. I might have looked sideways once in a while—and it was there, still staring hard at me. What's come over it now? It has vanished without a qualm, no permission asked for, as if we had never known each other before.

WOMAN. Forget it! It makes no difference.

HE. True. It doesn't. But I can't bear the idea of living without it. Even the loss of a limb is OK. One manages somehow. But how can you live without your reflection, even if it is useless?

WOMAN. Don't allow such thoughts to enter your mind. Allow only good thoughts.

HE. What do you mean allow? Do you think thoughts are sheep or cattle to be brought in by their ears?

WOMAN. Aayya! Why should you think of cattle and sheep? You're the limit. You are young. Your mind should have thoughts befitting a young man. As our Rigveda says: Let noble thoughts come to me from all directions.

HE. Huh! Vedas in 1984! Did these Veda chaps ever face a problem like mine?

WOMAN. Well then, there's a modem song which runs:

> The doors of two minds are open,
> The spring breeze lashes around.

HE. Sorry. That won't do for me.

WOMAN. Why don't you try? The one who tries, succeeds . . .

HE. Is my problem going to be solved by rattling off quotations?

WOMAN. It may, you know. It will, actually. One should be prepared for every-thing. You shouldn't reject anything. The window of the mind should be kept open—always.

HE. Great!

WOMAN. Really, why don't you do one thing? Let's try it out. You tell me no thoughts enter your mind. Suppose I enter your mind. What do you say to that? (*Coyly*) Let's watch what happens. Now this window . . . It's the window to your mind, right? If I come through there, I enter your mind. Then there is fun and nothing but fun. Great jubilation. Joy, oh what joy!

Just try, and you'll forget all that nonsense about your reflection. Agreed? Then it's agreed. Hunh? I am coming. Keep the window open. (*She hurries out of the door. He stares numbly at the closed window. A little while later there are fumbling sounds at the window. Then thumping, pushing and a high-pitched voice calling, 'Blockhead', 'Blockhead'. He doesn't move. Then the Woman uses a bit of muscle and shoves the window open.*) Whew! How tightly closed the window of your mind was! Don't you ever open it? The hinges have quite rusted away. (*She climbs on to the windowsill and tries to enter. The window is too narrow for her. She has to wriggle and squeeze her way in. At last she is through, and falls on the bed near the window with a thud. She is panting.*) Oh dear! The window of your mind is so narrow. How can splendid, magnificent thoughts ever enter it? I made it, though. And fell gently on your bed itself. (*She blushes. and laughs. She's wearing a flimsy nightie over her saree. She goes to him on tiptoe, like someone trying to stop her anklets from tinkling. Then she stamps her foot lightly to draw his attention. He is unmoved. Again she stamps her foot lightly. He's still unmoved. Then she leaps in the air and comes down with a thudding of both feet on the floor.*) Kis soch mein dube huwe ho? Kya mujhse koi galti ho gayi? Mujhse naraz to nahin? Chalo hum Kashmir jayenge . . .*

HE. For god's sake, woman . . .

WOMAN. Woman no more . . . I'm Hema Malini and you Dharmindar. I'm Suvarnamalini and you're Sootshekhar . . . I'm . . .†

HE. Oh Bai, will you please stop for a little while?

---

* 'What thought are you lost in? Have I done something wrong? Are you angry with me? Come, let's go to Kashmir.'

† Hema Malini (b. 1948): popular Indian actress of the 1970s and 80s. Dharminder: Refers to Dharmendra (b. 1935), also an Indian film star of the 1960s and 70s. They were a popular screen pair as well as a married couple in real life. Suvarnamalini and Sootsekhar: traditional Ayurvedic medicines.

WOMAN. No, no, no. I'm not stopping. The stopper's the loser. What dreams I've brought to your mind! Now let's both get lost in them. (*Sings.*) O my dreambuds!

HE (*shouts*). Stop it, Bai.

WOMAN. Oh, how loud you shout! Don't you know that the walls of the mind are fragile?

HE. Stop this drama.

WOMAN. But in your mind . . .

HE. It's my mind, isn't it?

WOMAN. Yes.

HE. And you've come into it.

WOMAN. Yes.

HE. Then how can you decide what should happen in my mind? Eh? It's you who are singing, you who are dancing, you who are deciding to go to Kashmir! As for me, I'm not even going to office today. You can't take charge of my mind like that. Out. Get out. Out. Get out.

WOMAN. But—but won't you listen to me?

HE. Out. Get out. Come on! I said, out! (*She moves towards the door.*) Not that way. (*Points to the window.*) Go out the way you came in.

She somehow manages to squeeze herself out of the window. Soon after, she enters through the door.

WOMAN (*cunning*). So, what happened in your mind?

HE. Oh, this and that.

WOMAN. Please tell me. What happened after I entered your mind?

HE. Why should I?

WOMAN. Was it something you can't talk about?

HE. Don't you know?

WOMAN. Really! How would I know what's in your mind?

HE. Come on.

WOMAN. Yes, how?

HE (*threatening*). Just let me enter your mind and I'll show you how.

WOMAN. Ooh! D'you really want to enter my mind? Really? Why ever didn't you tell me all these days?

HE. Because I didn't want to all these days. But I want to now.

WOMAN. Come then. Come. Come quickly. And do wear that red, dotted tie when you come. You look great in it. (*Hands over the tie.*) Hmm. Wear it. Go on. Come in now.

HE. Look out!

WOMAN. Hurry up. I really can't bear to wait.

HE. OK! I'll show you.

He goes out of the door. She waits, excited, eager like a sixteen-year-old.

WOMAN. Yoohoo. Have you come? Come, quick. The window's open. Come in straight. Oh, I hope you've not slipped from the balcony. How long will you keep me waiting?

HE. Can you hear me?

He leaps in through the window, roaring like a tiger. Looks around. Roars again.

WOMAN. Why do you roar? You look like the MGM lion.

HE. Silence!

WOMAN. The play is in session!*

---

* A reference to *Shantata! Court Chalu Aahe* (*Silence! The Court Is in Session*), a Marathi play by Vijay Tendulkar, first performed in 1971 and based on Friedrich Dürrenmatt's *Traps* (1956).

HE. Will you stop interrupting?

WOMAN. And do what? Bah! What a face you're making! Even paper tigers are better.

HE. I'll tear you apart and devour you.

WOMAN. Go, jump. Talking of devouring me. Go, take a look at yourself in a mirror. (*He roars angrily.*) Oh my god! He can't see his face in the mirror. How could I forget that? (*He roars.*) Oh, drop dead. You want to be a tiger? And do you think I'm any less? Arrey, if you're a tiger, I am a tigress. If you're an urban one, I'm a wild one. Do you follow? Hunh? (*She roars. His legs begin to tremble. He musters up courage and roars again. She roars. He roars. This continues till He begins to cough.*) Have a cough drop, Mr Tiger.

HE. Hey, you tigress! Just you wait. If you're the tigress, I'm the ringmaster. Get back. Back, I say. (*Mimes a whiplash in the air.*)

WOMAN. Oh, yeah. But the last item's still left, Mr Ringmaster. I'll open my jaws and you stick your head in. Come. (*Roars. Opens her mouth and walks up to him. Terrified, He moves back.*)

WOMAN. Why do you walk backwards? I too brush my teeth with toothpaste. People wouldn't want to put their heads in otherwise, would they? (*Roars.*)

He loses his balance. Continues walking backwards while she roars and advances until He jumps out of the window and runs away. A while later He comes in through the door.

HE (*shouting*). This isn't fair.

WOMAN. Now what's the matter?

HE. When *you* enter my mind, you're the one to decide what happens in it. Then when *I* enter yours, it's you again who decides. This is patently unfair. I seem to have no voice in the matter.

WOMAN. What can *I* do about it?

HE. It's absolutely immoral.

WOMAN. There's nothing unfair or immoral about it. My willpower just happens to be stronger than yours. What can I do about that? And what can you do about your willpower being so weak? Get beaten. Get pushed around. Get trampled upon.

HE. Yes. And go lose your reflection!

WOMAN. Quite. If you want to hold on to what you have, you've got to fight back in this world.

HE. Fight whom?

WOMAN. I couldn't tell you that. Fight means fight. Fight even the wind. I fight even with myself.

HE. Fight yourself?

WOMAN. Why not? I not only fight myself, I also sing to myself and talk to myself. Not that I can sing. But I still sing to myself. I go off tune even when I'm singing to myself, of course. And the lovely chats I have with myself. You just enter your own mind, make yourself comfortable and settle down to a good chat. Why don't you try it?

HE. Try what?

WOMAN. Entering your own mind. You think I'm unfair to you. So leave me out of it. Enter your own mind. Maybe you'll find your reflection there.

HE. In my mind?

WOMAN. Sure. You'll be surprised at the things you can find in your mind. All you need to do is look. Things you've lost, forgotten, discarded, thrown away. Things you don't want and do want, the modern, the ancient, the brand new, things turned to sawdust with white ants—try doing it, you must have this experience. It's like Alladin's treasure.

HE. Really?

WOMAN. I'm telling you.

HE. Shall I try?

WOMAN. You must. Would you like me to go with you to keep you company?

HE. No, certainly not.

WOMAN. Oh, I offer to go because it's your first time.

HE. No, no.

WOMAN. Well, then, what do I care?

HE. Will you go out now? I want to try.

WOMAN. Sure, sure. And—good luck. (*She goes out through the door.*)

> He thinks for a few moments, then He also leaves by the door. In a little while, He comes in through the window. The light dims until only a hazy spot remains on him. The rest is darkness, and a heavy strained silence. All of a sudden the phone starts to ring. Soon the alarm joins in. Then the doorbell. His breathing grows heavy. The spot on him disappears. The stage is unbelievably dark. Suddenly all three bells stop ringing. A terrible, tense silence, followed by a terrified scream. The sound of somebody stumbling about. Then silence. A moment later the lights come on. The stage is empty. He comes in through the door followed by the Woman.

WOMAN. I'd said, be careful, it's the first time . . .

HE. There's nothing there.

WOMAN. How can it be?

HE. That's the truth.

WOMAN. Don't lie.

HE. Just darkness. And deep silence. Like a graveyard. (*Silence.*) Please switch something on—the radio, anything. I can't bear the silence.

The Woman switches on the radio and turns the knobs. There's a lot of babble and crackle.

WOMAN. Is that better? (*He nods.*) Do you want it louder? (*Turns up the volume. In a moment the ads begin. The telephone, doorbell and alarm clock ring at the same time. She continues blabbering, her voice rising above the cackle, shrill and high.*) I can't understand why you don't like silence. Do you know how noise pollution has increased lately? Mind you, pollution has its advantages, though. People never see them. Actually, we should let every pollutant enter. You will want to know how. I thought you would. So let me explain. With illustrations. We used to have a car in the old days, see? When my husband was alive, see? Bought it second-hand. It was so old, you couldn't buy spare parts for it in the market. That's the kind of car it was. But my husband used to drive it around, not one bit bothered. And the car used to run, quite happily. Never needing servicing or repairing. It always puzzled me as to how it ran at all. So one day I asked my husband, and he says—do you know what he says?—It's simple, he says. It's simple. When you don't clean the car, all the parts remain stuck together tight. But the minute you clean it, the parts become loose, rattle and fall off. So you see—are you feeling a little better now? (*He nods. As her speech proceeds, the other noises have petered off and died down. Only her voice and the doorbell continue till she stops talking, leaving only the doorbell ringing away.*) What bell is that? Someone at the door, I think. (*She opens the door. A man enters. Delighted.*) Come in, Mr Flags, you're right on time.

FLAGS. So you've not had your breakfast yet? I left home without breakfast too.

WOMAN. Stop talking about breakfasts. What a morning it's been for us! Mr Blockhead has . . .

FLAGS. So Blockhead's playing hookie from work, eh?

WOMAN. Mr Blockhead has . . .

FLAGS. Bastards. The minute you become an officer, corruption gets into you. Our union is planning a front against shirkers like you.

WOMAN. Mr Blockhead . . .

FLAGS. And what are you doing wearing a tie at home? Lungi below, tie above? Hybrid officers like you should be pushed into the sea. A bit of money in hand, and they're in a hurry to forget their roots.

WOMAN. Block . . .

FLAGS. Why are you going block-block all the time? Can't you let us talk?

HE (*suddenly*). Flags, I've lost my reflection.

FLAGS. So?

WOMAN (*in great excitement*). That's what I say. You see, he realized it this morning. It was like this. I came into the room with a broom and a cup of tea. And he wandered into the bathroom brushing his teeth. Actually, I hate people wandering around brushing their teeth. There's a way to brush the teeth, you have to bend carefully over the basin. Anyway, he wandered around and then stood looking in the mirror, brushing his teeth—and then . . . the way he screamed, I can't describe it. As if somebody had taken his life's savings. I said to him: What's happened? And he comes out shaking like a leaf and says he can't see his reflection. What fun!

FLAGS (*yawns*). Get me a cup of tea, please. You make such excellent tea. Pure nectar.

WOMAN. Sure, why just tea . . . I can get you some toast and eggs as well.

FLAGS. That's what I call a big heart. The right spirit. Not like this wet rag here, sitting with his head in his hands, all limp and nervous. Just because his reflection's disappeared. (*She smirks and goes out.*)

HE. You too, Flags!

FLAGS. Me too what?

HE. Such a precious possession . . .

FLAGS. I don't believe in private property.

HE. Don't you understand my sorrow?

FLAGS. If you are going to sorrow over all the wrong and trivial things, who is going to sympathize with you?

HE. Is losing one's reflection a trivial thing according to you?

FLAGS. Blocks, do you know that, in this city alone, 99 per cent of the people live below the reflection line? Who listens to their complaint? Only the petty-bourgeois like you go whining about things like that. You're really terrible people—selfish and self-centred. Constantly thinking of yourselves and your reflections. Arrey, why the hell do you need this worthless reflection? You're not such an Adonis that you should have a pretty reflection. Blocks, don't get angry if I tell you the truth. But when you're not actually before me, I just can't remember what you look like. However hard I try, I see just a vague shape. With eyes and nose and ears. That's not surprising. You're like a million or ten million other people. What would there be that's worth remembering in you, dear Blockhead? So why bother with fancy things like reflections? One wouldn't find you in a crowd if one tried. A crowd—that's the thing. What's one puny individual? And what difference will it make to the world if you've lost your reflection? What? Speak!

HE. OK! It won't make any difference. But . . .

FLAGS. Of course it won't. Stop worrying. Shave and go off to work in style.

HE. But Flags, suppose everybody loses his reflection? What would happen then?

FLAGS. What would happen?

HE. Wouldn't it cause an upheaval? People would be frightened, furious. They would riot.

FLAGS. Nothing of the kind!

HE. Wouldn't they!

FLAGS. Never. It's very simple. How many people are really conscious that they have a reflection? People in this city sweat away at their work from morning to night. They don't have the time even to wipe their sweat in front of mirrors. How do you think it's going to affect them even if they did lose their reflection? Only you conceited highbrow types can afford that luxury. And just suppose that everyone, every single person, loses his reflection— then it's perfect, I say. It'll be the realization of the dream we've struggled for night and day. Equality will be established. Inequality destroyed. Everyone reduced to a single class. Splendid! What more would one want?

WOMAN (*through the window*). We would want tea. Want toast. Want eggs. (*Disappears.*)

FLAGS. Want, want, want . . .

HE. What's happened to you, all of a sudden?

FLAGS. The breakfast. My mind's full of it.

HE. But weren't you sermonizing on thoughts just the opposite?

FLAGS. Thoughts from the soul, all of them. I speak them out even in my sleep.

HE. Parrot-like!

FLAGS. Do you mean to say that I talk like a parrot?

HE. Yes, you do. You'll know when you lose your reflection.

FLAGS. Rubbish.

HE. What is rubbish?

FLAGS. Why should I lose it?

HE. You can never tell.

FLAGS. Nonsense!

HE. For all you know, it's already lost.

FLAGS. What rot!

HE. These are bad days. You'd better make sure. Better take care of it.

FLAGS (*uneasy*). If it's lost, it's lost! If others have lost theirs and I haven't, I'll smash it up myself. You hear? Just remember, we are committed to our ideology.

HE. Why don't you have a look anyway?

FLAGS. What for?

HE. Just have a look.

FLAGS. OK. I'll do it. Just to satisfy you . . . (*Walks over to the mirror and peers at it but turns away almost at once.*) It's there.

HE. What's there?

FLAGS. My reflection. It's there. (*A sigh of relief.*) That's that.

HE. Yes. Go on, lie.

FLAGS. Come and have a look for yourself. Come, you won't see yourself in any case. Come.

Both go to the mirtor and stand before it. He roars with laughter.

FLAGS. What's so funny? Stop neighing.

HE. You call that a reflection?

FLAGS. It *is* a reflection.

HE. Haw-haw-haw, hee-hee-hee . . . (*He rolls on the carpet.*)

The Woman comes in with tea and toast.

WOMAN. Oh! So you've found your reflection?

HE. Ho-ho-ho!

WOMAN. It's back in the mirror, is it? So the real celebration is on! Hadn't I told you . . .

HE. Bai, aho bai, it's really the limit, you know.

WOMAN. Why the limit? Didn't I tell you, it must have got bored and gone out for some fresh air or to take a piss. It'll come back? Where could it go, after all?

HE. No, no, no. You've got it all wrong. We're not talking about my reflection.

WOMAN. No?

HE. No, it still hasn't come back.

WOMAN. Oh!

HE. We're talking about his reflection. We just saw it. Ho-ho-ho.

FLAGS. Stop it, Blocks! Reflectionless slob!

WOMAN. Will you please tell me what's going on?

HE. No. No. You tell. Go and have a look, and tell.

WOMAN. Really?

HE. Yes. Go and have a look. Go. Go on, Flags. Go, stand in front of the mirror once more.

WOMAN. Come, come.

FLAGS. What childishness is this!

HE. Hey, coward! Scared, huh?

FLAGS. Why should I be scared? Eh? Why should I be scared?

HE. Then why don't you go to the mirror? Go. (*To the Woman*) Bai. now you can come and have a look.

Flags and the Woman go to the mirror. The Woman instantly blushes to the roots of her hair. She covers her eyes.

WOMAN. Oooh! My!

HE. What did you see? What did you see?

WOMAN. You're really naughty.

HE. What's naughty about it?

WOMAN. Of course, it's naughty. Quite wicked. Both of you.

HE. Naughty? Wicked? Don't blush. What did you see in the mirror? What did you see?

WOMAN. I'm not going to tell. No. No, I won't.

HE. What did you see? Shall I tell you?

WOMAN (*puts her fingers in her ears*). Go ahead.

HE. I saw a cock. I saw him reflected as a cock.

WOMAN (*taking her fingers out of her ears*). Did you? You too?

HE. You mean you saw it too?

WOMAN. You really did see a co-co-co. (*Giggles.*) I didn't know you were one of that kind.

HE. That kind?

WOMAN. Those that like Co-co-hu-hu-hu—

HE. No, no. Who told you I like cocks? So, this cock of ours is crowing his little bit over and over again . . .

WOMAN. Crowing his little bit? What cock are you talking about?

HE. What cock?

WOMAN. But when you say 'cock', don't you mean that (*rolls her eyes significantly*) . . . well . . .

HE. Of course I mean this cock, that cock, any cock when I say cock. Now all cocks strut around and crow, don't they?

WOMAN. Oh, that. That's not what I saw.

HE. No. What did you see then?

WOMAN. I didn't see the bird. Not the one you're talking of.

HE. What did you see then?

WOMAN. Now, how can I say that? I feel so very very shy. You know Dilip Chitre, and his play *Mithu Mithu Popat*? Don't you remember the symbolic bird in it? Well, that's what I saw in the mirror.

FLAGS. No, that's enough. Enough. Saw a cock now, didn't you? OK, it was a cock, after all. You saw something at least. Not the blank that someone here faces. (*He crows like a cock.*) Doesn't bother me one bit. (*Again, He crows like a cock.*)

WOMAN. Please stop it. The cock must be quite hungry. Would you care to eat something? Here's your toast. And tea. And eggs.

He crows.

FLAGS. You unbeliever! I'll finish you off, just wait.

HE. How?

FLAGS. Kill you. Annihilate you. Purge, liquidate.

HE. How would that help, Mr Cock?

FLAGS. It's people like you who are the enemies of revolution. Once you are eliminated, the path of revolution will be smooth.

HE. It won't.

FLAGS. It will.

HE. Never. Because even if you destroy us, we'll enter your minds. What will you do, then?

FLAGS. That's impossible.

HE. We'll enter your minds and torture you. Give you feelings of guilt. Guilt complex!

FLAGS. Pooh! You don't have the guts!

HE. Want to see? OK, then, I'll show you, old Flagstaff! (*Runs out of the door.*)

WOMAN. He's gone bonkers. Don't let him bother you. Come, start eating.

  He peeps in through the window.

HE. May I come in?

FLAGS. No. No.

HE. I'm coming.

FLAGS. Nor while I'm having my breakfast.

HE. Coming. Coming. Coming.

  He comes in through the window.

WOMAN. Do eat. Would you like me to feed you ? Here. Have some toast. (*He sits down in front of Flags.*) Would you like me to feed you? Here, take some words. Here's some toast. (*Puts toast into Flags's mouth.*)

HE. Here's some commitment. (*Mimes feeding action*)

WOMAN. Egg. (*Same action.*)

HE. Exploitation. (*Same action.*)

WOMAN. Tea. (*Same action.*)

HE. Capitalism. (*Same action.*)

WOMAN. Toast. (*Same action.*)

HE. Class Struggle. (*Same action.*)

WOMAN. Egg. (*Same action.*)

HE. Blood. (*Same action.*)

WOMAN. Tea. (*Same action.*)

HE. Revolution. (*Same action.*)

WOMAN. Toast. (*Same action.*)

HE. The masses. (*Same action.*)

FLAGS. Enough, enough, enough. I'm full.

HE. Have some more.

FLAGS. No, I can't.

HE. How can you be full so soon? I've cooked for you our favourite words. Eat some more.

FLAGS. I can't. I'll burst.

HE. Why should you burst? Store them all up in your stomach. Then you can bring them up when you want. Like a camel. There.

FLAGS. You bloody reactionary! You enter my mind and dare provoke me! If I entered your mind, I'd make it real bad for you, I promise you.

HE. Balls.

FLAGS. I'll show you, just you wait.

HE. Yes, yes. Show me, show.

FLAGS. OK, then. Here goes. (*Flags leaves by the door*)

WOMAN. Dear me! This is going to be a real mess. Blockhead's in Flags's mind and now Flags is trying to get into Blockhead's. So A enters B which is already in A!

Flags is at the window.

HE. Don't you bite off more than you can chew. You'll get a fright at the end.

FLAGS. Pooh! Pooh!

Flags bangs his head on the window trying to come in. Finally manages it. Instant darkness. Flags screams. Sounds of someone stumbling around.

HE. Don't say I didn't warn you.

FLAGS. God! How dark it is in here.

HE. Yell now!

FLAGS. Hey, how do I get out of here?

HE. Sit and whine! I'm off.

The stage lights up. He comes in through the door.

FLAGS (*groping in the dark*). Hey! You've got out of my mind but I'm still stuck in yours. Help! Help!

HE. Bother! Now have you got your sense back?

FLAGS. Help! Help me get free.

HE. Hold on. Bloody nuisance. (*He goes out by the door and comes in through the window. Darkness.*) OK. Now off you go. Move your arse, will you? Easy, or you'll bump your head again.

Sounds of stumbling. Light. Flags enters through the door.

FLAGS. Whew, I'm out! That was a nasty one. Blocks, better leave my mind now.

HE. Say 'give up'.

FLAGS. OK, I give up.

HE. Now, that's better.

He steps out of the window and comes in through the door.

FLAGS (*furious*). Your types are like snakes in the grass. I must work out some instant measures. (*Goes out of the door muttering.*) Those who indulge in the luxury of private joys and sorrows (*looks in at the window*) have no right to be living in this world. You are the enemies of the people. The enemies of revolution. You

He gets up irritated and slams the window shut, probably catching Flags's nose because you hear Flags scream outside.

HE. Thank God, that's over. Now I can relax.

WOMAN. Aren't you going to shave first?

HE. What for?

WOMAN. To go to work. It's almost 8.30.

HE. I'm taking French leave today.

WOMAN. How can you take so many French leaves?

HE. For all you know, my reflection's already there.

WOMAN. Where?

HE. In the office. It must have been really keen to go. So it went off. And here I am, looking all over for it. I refuse to go now.

WOMAN. And if the boss calls?

HE. Why should he? With my reflection there, nobody will even notice I'm not. Don't forget, it's a government office.

WOMAN. Even so, I wish you'd shave.

HE. All right. (*Goes to the mirror.*) Hey. You're crazy. How do I shave?

WOMAN. Oh my! That's true.

HE. Great! Another bore I'm through with. Hurray!

WOMAN. You sound cheerful.

HE. Laugh, laugh, so that you don't cry.

WOMAN. Laugh, laugh. Life is meant to be filled with laughter.

HE. That's very true. Whatever happens, go on laughing. I've got my freedom now. Freedom. You know how a sack feels once it's relieved of all the grain? That's the kind of freedom I now have. It's my Independence Day today. I must sing my song of freedom.

He stands up looking extremely solemn.

HE (*sings*). *Tanamanadhana soduni gele, gele maja pratibimba.* *

WOMAN (*screams*). Stop it. Stop it at once.

HE. What's wrong?

WOMAN. Not that tune.

HE. Why not?

WOMAN. It's an insult to the national anthem, don't you know? You're not Raja Dhale to do that.

HE. You're right.

WOMAN. Set it to a classical tune. It'll sound lovely.

HE. OK. Classical it will be! Listen. It's the raga Kalavati.

(*Sings*)

> It has gone
> My reflection
> And so to hell
> With boss and fat woman
> Bosom pal and politician
> I'm through with them all
> No worry remains
> But to exist on and on.

Ahaha! What bliss in this freedom! What a sense of liberation! How can I describe its grandeur, its glory? Let's distribute sweets. We're free.

Let's take leave. We're free.

---

* 'It has left my body and soul, it's gone, my reflection.'

Drink, gamble, take bribes, We're free.

Go naked, go bare, eat, shit, We're free.

Do just what you like, who is to stop you?

Nobody to stare from the mirror in anger.

Cry if you like, laugh if you like.

Live if you like, die if you like.

WE'RE FREE, WE'RE FREE, WE'RE FREE!

Aah! What a great feeling. Beautiful darkness. around me. Darkness without. Darkness within. This is that moment of darkness. This is the knowledge of the self. The knowledge of life. The ultimate revelation. (*Sings*) *Aji me Brahma pahile.* *

The organ accompanies the song as in traditional Marathi musical plays. He continues the song till the doorbell rings.

HE. There it tolls. The bell tolls. That's the last bell tolling. Who could it be? Bai. Bai, open the door.

WOMAN. Wait till I've powdered my nose.

HE. Bai. Bai, open the door.

WOMAN. Wait till I've pinned up my hair.

HE. Bai. Bai, open the door.

WOMAN. Wait till my heart stops pounding.

(*A woman's sweet voice singing outside.*)

Oh, King of Clerks!

Rage has set the world on fire.

The sages laugh.

Let the rains pour.

---

* 'I've seen [Lord] Brahma today.'

The Woman opens the door to let in a young girl.

HE. Who is this, Muktabai, come to us?

GIRL. Namaskar.

HE. Who are you?

GIRL. You don't know me.

HE. That's why I ask you. Who are you?

GIRL. Do I have a name?

HE. What do you mean?

GIRL. It means I do not have a name. No name. But people at home, or outside, at the office, they all call me Broomstick.

HE. Broomstick?

GIRL. Yes. They're all dying to use me. (*Pause.*) Only you are different.

HE. Where do I come in?

GIRL. Very much.

HE. Now, now don't you drag me into something stupid.

WOMAN. Quite right. You better be careful.

GIRL. How are you not concerned? Don't we work in the same office, in the same section, in the same comer?

HE. I wouldn't know.

GIRL. What's wrong with you?

HE. Fifty girls to a section. They all wear synthetic sarees. They all wear perfume. They all use lipstick. How am I supposed to remember them all?

GIRL. You have a point.

HE. You look quite sensible. I guess you are yet to marry!

GIRL. You're right.

HE. All girls are tolerant, sensible and humble before marriage. But the moment they hook a husband, they start pontificating on liberation. By the way, did you come in by the door or through the window?

GIRL. The door. Why?

HE. I was scared for a moment. That's all.

GIRL. But why?

HE. If you came in by the window, I want you to leave the same way, this moment . . .

GIRL. I've not come today to go away.

HE. What?

WOMAN. Look, I'm not having girls staying here. Suppose something goes wrong?

GIRL. In that case I'll take him away.

HE. Where?

GIRL. Anywhere.

HE. And where's that?

GIRL. Just anywhere. Anywhere in this wide world. I could go to the end of the earth with you.

HE. Why should you?

GIRL (*very sentimentally*). Now how am I tell you this? I love you. It's a silent love. I've gazed at you in the office with such longing for so long. How handsome you look—the incoming files to your right, the outgoing files to your left, their dusty yellow colour, the old table, the inkpot, the pen-holder, the paperweight, the calendar on the wall with the picture of an adivasi girl dangling her feet in the water, and Mrs Gandhi's photograph, the Godrej cupboard. The records tied in red cloth to the left, and beyond that the broken door of the toilet which does not bolt. In the midst of all this, you, the lord of my heart, looking so good, so right, like the sun shining at the centre of the nine planets, like candy among popcorn, like a shining boot in a heap of old slippers.

HE. Have you been reading a lot of stories by the Marathi women writers?

GIRL. Why?

HE. Or has the heroine of a story stepped out to make an appearance here? (*The Girl shakes her head.*) Eh? (*The Girl shakes her head again.*) If you're one of those heroines, let me tell you that the trend has changed. Nowadays, the husbands of heroines live in Tokyo or Zurich or Rome and earn fat pay packets. The heroines fall in love with Japanese, Swiss or Italian men, depending on where the husbands are posted. There's a lot of romancing all over the place, with the husbands knowing exactly what's going on. The husbands endure it all like the traditional Aryan pativratas. * Then the 'phoren'.† Romeos get bored with the heroines and ditch them. The heroines return to their native husbands and sob their broken hearts out while the husbands say, 'there, there,' and make them cups of coffee. So you see? The heroines of Marathi stories have started philandering. The moment they sight a lone man, they pounce. In short, I'd advise you to get married to feel liberated. Then you won't need to talk sentimentally like this. You will be militant then, and talk about women's lib.

GIRL. Please. Do you think I don't mean what I say?

HE. Tell me what you've come here for.

GIRL. Would you like to know the truth?

HE. Yes. Please.

GIRL. I found out you'd lost your reflection.

---

* Pativrata: A married woman who is loyal to her husband.
† Phoren: Foreign, but used mockingly in Hindi accent.

HE. What?

GIRL. Yes.

HE. How did you find out?

GIRL. I did. Don't you remember the day you were looking at the mirror above the washbasin in the canteen? You were looking quite half-heartedly, so you didn't notice it. But there was no reflection.

HE. How did you know?

GIRL. I was standing right behind you.

HE. Don't tell lies.

GIRL. Cross my heart, I was.

HE. Now uncross your heart.

GIRL. OK. I will.

HE. Leave me out. If you were behind me, why was your reflection not there in the mirror?

GIRL. How could there be?

HE. Why?

GIRL. I've lost my reflection too.

He looks stunned.

HE. You're lying.

GIRL. No, honest. I hadn't noticed till one day Mother got furious. I've been watching you for days, she says. Why can't you wear the kumkum* in its proper place? Sometimes it is there, sometimes it is not. When it's there, it's on your cheek or your nose! What's got into you? We women have to guard our kumkum with our lives. Both before and after marriage.

---

* Red pigment used by Hindu women to make a round mark on the forehead.

WOMAN. Very true. When my husband was alive, I used to wear a teeny-weeny dot. Because he was such a beanpole. Now I don't have to bother.

GIRL. So I took the kumkum out of my handbag and went to the mirror. And guess what? I couldn't see a thing. I just put the kumkum approximately where I thought it should be. And the mirror showed just this dot. It really scared me, but I didn't say a thing. I didn't mind losing my reflection as long as my kumkum was safe.

HE. Terrific! Shake hands.

WOMAN. Oh no, you won't. (*To the Girl*) Now scram.

HE. Don't say that. We're comrades in sorrow—or in joy. When a broom comes into the house, Dusserah must follow.

WOMAN. She's taking you for a ride. Don't trust her.

HE. Why do you say that?

WOMAN. It's an old trick we women use. Tears. And if she is telling the truth, then your tragedy is no longer unique. Your monopoly is gone.

HE. Yes! You're right!

GIRL. Don't you believe me?

HE. Whether I do or don't—what difference will it make to me? (*Suspicious.*) Look here. Are you laying some kind of trap for me?

GIRL. Trap?

HE. Have you knowingly hidden your reflection somewhere? In a bank vault or a false ceiling in the bathroom?

GIRL. What? Do you think a reflection is like a film star's black money?

HE. Or have you gifted it to someone on an impulse or because you were fed up with it? And now you cry thief. Bai's right. It's a trick to win sympathy.

Huh! I don't feel a bit sympathetic. You'd better go away. Go and look after your problem and I'll look after mine.

GIRL. How impersonal a man without reflection becomes. How hard-hearted! How amoral! Amoral, I said—not immoral.

HE. Don't show off your intellectualism with your fine moral judgements. I'm through with all labels now, thank god!

GIRL. How un-responsible! Not irresponsible, but un-responsible.

HE. Did you do your Masters in linguistics, by any chance?

GIRL. Yes. With philosophy. How else could I have got into the Accounts Section? We could do our thing.

HE. We?

GIRL. I'm a girl, after all. What can I do alone? Help me. And I'll help you. We are both people who have lost our reflections. We could help each other find them.

HE. Oh—you find mine, I find yours.

GIRL. Yes.

HE. Or each find his own.

GIRL. But together.

HE. Sorry. Can't be done.

GIRL. Why not? Hasn't it been said that the two wheels of the carriage of life—

HE. What carriages are you talking about? Talk of spaceships. Soyuz. Here we are, drifting alone in space, weightless, reflectionless.

GIRL. But the two of us?

HE. Now not a thing more. This doing things together is yet another old trick. The two of us together will fight for freedom. The two of us together will abolish inequality. The two of us together will serve society. The two of us together will set up an ashram for celibates. Nothing doing, sorry. It all ends up in breeding brats. Now, look, both of us being what we are, what do we achieve by begetting children without reflections? And what about their future? Set them adrift in space? To go floating about, all by themselves, without a direction, a drift? To float in the ocean of joy, bursting into ripples of joy? No, thanks. We're lucky—we got free by chance. Why give birth to new prisoners? Eh?

GIRL. I really can't fathom your mind.

HE. Why should you want to? Really, you women have some ambition!

GIRL. All I ask for is a little corner of your mind to rest my tired head in. To help me forget my grief over my lost reflection.

HE. Good lord! What a range this girl covers! She is the LCM of all heroines in Marathi fiction.

WOMAN. Range my foot! She's a leech. Really, how sticky can you get. Now. hold your lovey-dovey nonsense.

GIRL. Give me a chance. Only one, I beg you.

HE. I tell you, there is total darkness in my mind. I can't see a thing there myself. Why do you want to go stumbling through that strange place?

GIRL. I'll light the lamp of my love in there and banish the darkness.

WOMAN. Light!

HE. But what do you get by lighting up that place? You won't see a thing there anyway. Besides, what's light and what's darkness for those who have lost their reflections? Everything remains the same.

GIRL. But you too . . . one who does not care either way . . . why should you be so obstinate about your mind?

HE. You've a point! OK. Go. Go into my mind since you're so keen.

GIRL. Go? You mean come. (*Turns to the door.*)

WOMAN. Leave your slippers outside, do you hear?

The Girl goes out.

HE. What a female! How can a person without a reflection be so optimistic?

WOMAN. Optimism is just another word for leechiness. (*The Girl returns*). Now what?

GIRL. I'm scared.

WOMAN. Naturally. The mind is

GIRL. It's not that. But suppose somebody closes the window while I'm inside?

WOMAN (*flares up*). Don't we have other things to do? And suppose it shuts, push it open. The hinges are all rusty anyway. (*The Girl begins to leave.*) And come out fast. Behave yourself while you're there. And don't scamper around there like a mouse in a trap.

The Girl goes out of the door.

HE. You people have turned my mind into a railway platform today—you and Flags and Broomsticks. (*The Girl opens the window gently and comes in. Stands in the middle of the stage. The darkness is total. There is a long silence, broken only by two sobs, followed by silence again The stage lights up. The Girl comes in through the door.*) Happy?

GIRL (*angry*). Are you?

HE. I'd warned you.

GIRL. How I sobbed in your mind! You could have spoken a few words of sympathy at least.

HE. But I didn't hear you.

WOMAN. Nor did I!

GIRL. Brutal. Heartless. Cruel.

HE. Bloody hell! It's the limit. That's the trouble with these suffering souls. They want the whole world to up its arse and blow on their wounds. Pains!

GIRL. You've never suffered. That's why you talk like this. You haven't suffered because you don't know what you've lost.

HE. Oh yes, I do, dear woman! I certainly do. But I know it's useless searching for what's lost. You don't agree. So go search. You and I are different. And our paths lie in opposite directions. Since we have this freedom to go our different ways, why don't we enjoy it?

GIRL. But the mind . . .

HE. The mind! Why don't you understand? Is there such a thing as the mind? And if there is, it's impossible to understand other people's. We read other minds in the context of our own. We see all kinds of meanings—desirable and undesirable—which have nothing to do with the other mind. They are all in our minds. You understand? I ask you because you are an MA in philosophy.

GIRL. What has it got to do with my being an MA in philosophy? I'm also a broomstick. You came into my mind, and you can see for yourself what I'm saying.

HE. Your mind? I suppose you have the works of Hegel and Kant there, so . . .

GIRL. Not at all. They weren't there even when I was doing my MA. Why don't you come and see?

HE. And do what?

WOMAN. Do nothing. Just talk.

GIRL. Just make sure . . .

WOMAN. There'll be no hanky-panky. Not in my house.

GIRL. . . . that you are not the only one with a mind. Other people may have a mind too . . .

HE. I'm really tired. I've been in and out of minds so many times today.

GIRL. This is my last request. I won't bother you after this.

WOMAN. Some favour, that.

HE. OK. But I'm not going to stand for any more nonsense after this. You'll have to release me.

GIRL. Yes.

He goes to the door.

WOMAN. Hey. Take off that tie. Why do you want to go all dolled up as if it was a wedding reception? (*He takes off his tie and goes out of the door. To the Girl*) Doesn't change his underwear for days.

He comes softly in through the window. Slowly makes his way to centrestage. The two are far apart. The stage is dark but for a faint light on the two of them.

HE. My dear girl, why play games? Aren't you tired of all this? Haven't we played this game a little too often in life? You have played it with some people, I with others. And it always ends the same way. What do we gain from it? Do we achieve anything? Love is stumbling around in each other's darkness. What's the use? What is wrong with our own darkness? You'll say: But there is the body. So there is. But the same darkness flows along the arteries too. If you cut yourself, a sticky black fluid oozes out. There's no ache. No pain. So much time has passed. My body has forgotten the touch of rain. And the scent of flowers. The warm smell of fresh bread, the moonlight above the lake, the ring of children's laughter, moist lips meeting passionately in the dark. I have them all preserved like dead butterflies pinned in a notebook Slowly they too will turn to dust. That's all right. All these things have vanished along with my reflection. I began losing them, one by one, long ago. But I didn't notice. So. Good. Now I don't have to worry about the future or the past or the present. Because all time is dark in the same way. And there is no difference between optimism and pessimism.

Let me tell you a story about a pair of lovers. Both were young and beautiful and intelligent. And passionately in love. They swore they would be together in this and all future lives. But soon they were separated. He went to the war and never returned. He was reported missing. Everybody said he must be dead. But she remained steadfast. She said he would return. For forty years she remained true to her word, and waited for him to return. One day she got a message: 'I've returned. Meet me in the temple at the end of the village.' She said, 'See. Didn't I say so?' And she ran. She reached the temple. But she couldn't see him. The only person there was an ancient man, toothless and bald and rheumy-eyed. She said: 'There's nobody here. Some young hoodlum has fooled me.' She went back, bitterly disappointed. The lover too got tired of waiting for her in the temple. Not a single creature turned up, except an old woman, bent, with matted hair and cataracts in her eyes. She peeped in briefly and went away, muttering, to herself. He was also disappointed: 'She hasn't waited. She's made a new life for herself. Didn't even come to meet me.'

After this only his lips are seen to move. Not a word is audible. Darkness. Light. Only the Woman is on the stage now. The Girl has disappeared. He comes in through the door.

WOMAN. She's gone. (*Only his lips move.*) She kept yawning and looking at her watch. (*Only his lips move.*) I can't hear anything at all. (*He stares at her. Then at the objects in the room. Then He calmly walks to the window. Climbs up. Jumps. The Woman runs to the window. Stands looking out. Turns back.*) Nothing wrong in killing yourself. But after falling five floors into the middle of the road without so much as a sound, or a bloodstain or a traffic pile up, something huge and black gushed out and spread on the road like oil. What kind of a death is that! Huh!

She closes the window. Turns the sheet on the bed. The doorbell rings and stops. She runs to the mirror, smoothing down her hair, then stands rooted before it. Staring at the mirror. Then turns to the audience with terror-stricken eyes. Then a never-ending scream breaks from her lips.

The doorbell goes on ringing as she screams.

Darkness.

Silence.

The audience leaves in the dark as the organ plays 'Aji me Brahma pahile'.

Curtain.

AUTOBIOGRAPHY

(Atmakatha)

TRANSLATED BY PRATIMA KULKARNI

Autobiography was performed for the first time in the original Marathi by RoopWedha at Experimental Theatre, National Centre for the Performing Arts, Bombay, on 25 September 1988, with the following cast:

ANANTRAO RAJADHYAKSHA [RAJA]	Dr Shreeram Lagoo
PRADNYA	Shubhangi Sangwai
UTTARA	Jyoti Subhaschandra
VASANTI	Suhas Joshi
DIRECTION	Pratima Kulkarni
SOUND	Sandeep Kshemakalyani
SETS	Shyam Bhutkar
LIGHTING	Kumar Sohoni

The stage is divided into three sections: A, B and C; A to the left, B to the right and C in the centre. A shows the study of a wealthy, sophisticated and successful writer: lots of books, a painting or two, a plush leather sofa with a tall lamp next to it and a cane stool in front. B suggests a comfortable drawing room; C is totally empty.

Evening has just fallen when the play opens, with some stars rising in the sky. As the play advances, more and more stars come into view, and, as the play ends, the sky dazzles with stars all over.

Curtain rises to show Rajadhyaksha (78) sitting on a sofa, Pradnya (22–24) on a cane stool. A tape recorder between the two.

RAJA. . . . Though Tilak died in 1920,* Gandhi had become popular around 1915. After 1920, people had begun to forget Tilak and his politics. The

---

* Bal Gangadhar Tilak (1856–1920), a radical nationalist, widely considered the first leader of the Indian Independence Movement. When Mahatma Gandhi returned to India from South Africa is 1915, Tilak tried to convince him to move away from his idea of total non-violence and requested him to seek self-rule through any means possible. Though Gandhi considered Tilak his guru, he did not change his mind and went on to lead the Independence Movement from the late 1910s onwards.

entire country was coming under the spell of Gandhi's thoughts and personality. The morality inherent in his political thinking and the spiritual foundation of that thinking was fascinating to the Indian mind. Writers, too, could not stay away from it. I started writing around 1930, and writing anything that was not linked with the national movement I found sacrilegious at that time. The word 'commitment' has come into being only in the last one decade. In our youth, we had not heard this word. But we were committed nonetheless to our national movement, to our idealism that came so naturally that we were not even aware of it. Idealism and commitment were not fashion in those days—they flowed in our blood . . .

PRADNYA (*switching off the recorder*). Wait . . .

RAJA. Now what?

PRADNYA. Let's check if it's recording . . .

RAJA. Must you keep doing this for ever? I lose my link every time.

PRADNYA. What's the great use of your link if it doesn't record?

RAJA. A smart, modern girl like you . . . can't you even operate a simple tape recorder?

Pradnya starts the recorder. The last two lines of Rajadhyaksha's speech are heard as playback.

PRADNYA. Yeah, it's OK. (*Putting it off as his speech ends*) Excellent! Continue . . .

RAJA. What?

PRADNYA. Go ahead!

RAJA. What was I saying?

PRADNYA. 'Idealism and commitment were not fashion in those days—they flowed in our blood . . .'

RAJA. Of course that's how it was.

PRADNYA. OK, OK! Go ahead!

RAJA. Not now.

PRADNYA. Why?

RAJA. No.

PRADNYA. But why?

RAJA. I've lost interest.

PRADNYA. How can you lose interest every two minutes?

RAJA. Why did you have to break my link?

PRADNYA. Keep looking for an excuse.

RAJA. Won't you ever think of my age? How can you be so cruel?

PRADNYA. Oh, I've thought of that. It's just the right age for someone to write one's autobiography. Don't waste time now. Or you'll be gone, leaving it half-done.

RAJA. Where?

PRADNYA. What do you mean, where . . . ?

RAJA. Huh! I'm just about nearing seventy.

PRADNYA. Don't conceal your age, mister! Not like women, I mean. But you men are just as vain. You completed seventy-eight this year in July. Your date of birth is 21 July 1908. Guru Purnima.

RAJA. Did you have to probe into my date of birth?

PRADNYA. It's my job! For my research on your work, I have to get your bio-data all correct.

RAJA. Research, like hell! What's a stupid ass like you going to get out of it? . . . Why don't you change your name? Pradnya is such a misnomer for a perfect idiot like you.

PRADNYA. OK, so I'm an idiot. Fine. But when I read your books, discerningly at that, and I thought: Such a bore, has to read in-between yawns . . .

RAJA. Some cheek!

PRADNYA. I realized I wasn't going to get my hands on anything there. Just some mushy idealism. That one, flowing in your blood . . .

RAJA. Cheek!

PRADNYA. Only your poems are real. Specially the earliest ones. Such intense, beautiful lyric poems . . . Almost ethereal. Where's all that gone now?

RAJA. Is this the beginning of another inquisition?

PRADNYA. Sorry. Shall we start? I'm switching it on.

RAJA. Why don't we have some tea? You make good tea, you know.

PRADNYA. Go on, pamper yourself.

RAJA. You started it. I never invited you; Come, come, pamper me . . .

PRADNYA. I had to fake all that, you see. You'd never have agreed to talk otherwise.

RAJA. Whatever, whatever. . . but now you're trapped.

PRADNYA. Trapped? That's true. You've got me trapped with this autobiography of yours . . .

RAJA. You lazybones! Do you realize how lucky you are? A celebrated, great writer like me, dictating his autobiography to you. To you! Do you realize what that means? Thousands would give anything for a chance like this.

PRADNYA. I'm not one of those, in any case.

RAJA. I'll put in a word of thanks to you in my Preface.

PRADNYA. I won't let you go at that.

RAJA. OK, now, tell me the truth. Don't you find my narrative interesting?

PRADNYA. Not one bit.

RAJA. No?

PRADNYA. Don't have such fascinating illusions.

RAJA. Then what made you . . .

PRADNYA. I agreed to take this on because it's going to be useful for my thesis. Purely ulterior motive, Padma Bhushan Rajadhyaksha!*

RAJA. What a heartless generation!

PRADNYA. But now I'm not even quite sure of its usefulness.

RAJA. I'm filling you in on such important information!

PRADNYA. But that's available anywhere. What's so new about what you're saying?

RAJA. Don't get cheeky.

PRADNYA. Firstly, when you talk about history, you're full of vague statements.

RAJA. Hmm.

PRADNYA. Let me make the tea.

RAJA. Sit down. What's vague about what I'm saying?

PRADNYA. I did this, I thought that . . . I mean, it's OK and all that, but what I did not do, why I did not do what I did not do—you just don't discuss such things, you don't even mention them!

---

* Padma Bhushan: The third-highest civilian award conferred by the Government of India.

RAJA. What was there I didn't mention?

PRADNYA. Mardhekar was almost your contemporary. You never mentioned him. He gave a new sensibility to the Marathi reader, whether you like it or not. But what do you think of his contribution? Or the Mardhekar wave just came and went and left you dry and unruffled?

RAJA. Mardhekar and I lived different lives. He was a bureaucrat. I was in the mainstream of the nationalist movement. I went to jail in 1942, I gave up my job, my security . . .

PRADNYA. Right. You speak of all these things—eloquently. Going to jail in '42 appears again and again. But why didn't you go to jail in '75? How did your idealism adapt itself to the Emergency?* . . . I mean, I have nothing to say if it did adapt—no value judgement—but if we knew why you did that, we may perhaps understand you better.

RAJA. Did any writer go to jail during the Emergency? All . . .

PRADNYA. Durgabai did.

RAJA. It was pointless to get holed up in jail. You could do so much by staying out. And we did that. Travelled all over Maharashtra for the Janata Party, making speeches.†

---

* A 21-month period from 1975 to 1977 when Prime Minister Indira Gandhi had a state of emergency declared across India. This gave the the prime minister the authority to rule by decree, allowing elections to be suspended and civil liberties to be curbed. Most of Mrs Gandhi's political opponents were imprisoned and the press was censored. The most controversial period of post-Independence India, the Emergency is still seen as a time of sweeping human rights violations.

† Literally 'People's Party', it refers to an amalgam of Indian political parties opposed to the Emergency (1975–77). In the general election held after the Emergency in 1977, the Janata Party defeated Indira Gandhi's Congress Party and formed the central government.

PRADNYA. But you still held on to your Padma Bhushan. Phanishwar Nath Renu did not.* You did not resign from the government committees.

RAJA. Are you trying to find fault with . . .

PRADNYA. No. I've said it already—no value judgement. But we must know what you did not do and why.

RAJA. How does that matter?

PRADNYA. It matters because if we understand you as a person, it may help my generation a little to make some sense of your writing. Perhaps!

RAJA. My writing is going to end with my generation, Pradnya.

PRADNYA. But it should not.

RAJA. I know. But it will, all the same. I know that for your generation, my work, if they read it at all, is dated, passe. (*Pause.*) At times it is passe even for me . . . You read it today for your research. There may be some five or ten other students. But who knows, after twenty years, will I even be remembered as a writer?

PRADNYA. Why is it so? (*Pause.*) How come you're so damned confident that you'll be forgotten? Why don't you explore this in your autobiography? You know, perhaps your success as a writer will be determined by this self-exploration? After all, isn't autobiography meant to be self-exploration? . . . Am I talking too much ? (*Pause.*) Did I hurt you? (*Pause.*) I didn't mean it that way. (*Pause.*) Please say something.

---

* Phanishwar Nath Renu (1921–77): One of the most successful and influential writers of modern Hindi literature and the author of *Maila Aanchal* (The Soiled Linen, 1954), which is regarded as one of the most significant Hindi novels. Honoured with the Padma Shri in 1970 by the Government of India, he returned the award in protest against the Emergency.

RAJA. I'm way beyond all that now. (*A clean laugh.*) I got everything in life, you see . . . Lots of honours, foreign trips, Padma Bhushan—yes! That leaves out only the Jnanpith.

PRADNYA. Four more years. You've got to be at least eighty for the Jnanpith. That's the main qualification.

RAJA. Oh, I'll get that too. There isn't much competition in the above-eighty category . . . When did these irrelevant factors become more important than writing? I didn't even notice.

PRADNYA. Then why don't you try to get to the root of these things? As a person, you are so frank and honest, but as a writer you're—

RAJA. Vague!

PRADNYA. Or you simplify things, steep them in imagination, at times glorify them. Doesn't the truth get smothered by all this?

RAJA. If I only knew what the truth was! Only then could I have answered your question.

PRADNYA. Uttarabai has published your letters. Do they or do they not tell the truth?

RAJA (*enraged*). You read those?

PRADNYA. I did.

RAJA. She has published them out of context. Only some, at that. Not all. And only mine. Where are the letters she wrote to me?

PRADNYA. I'm sorry.

RAJA. Why should you be sorry? The damned book is available at any corner, any roadside stall. I never thought Uttara could stoop so low.

---

* An Indian literary award presented annually to an author for their outstanding contribution towards literature. Widely regarded as the ultimate prize in Indian literature.

PRADNYA. She shouldn't have published them without your consent. I mean that. (*Pause.*)

RAJA. She did ask me.

PRADNYA. And when you didn't give . . .

RAJA. I did. (*Long pause.*)

PRADNYA. But the newspapers are bursting with controversies about . . .

RAJA. Is the recorder off?

PRADNYA (*looks at the recorder*). . . . whether she was justified or not justified in publishing those letters. There's a general impression that you were not aware of any such thing.

RAJA. Uttara telephoned.

PRADNYA. She did? On her own? Herself?

RAJA. She thought that was enough.

PRADNYA. Then why don't you explain?

RAJA. She should. It's her book.

PRADNYA. But you are being wronged. And does she have your consent in writing?

RAJA. I said we talked on the phone.

PRADNYA. Which means she has nothing to prove that she has your consent.

RAJA. But if she says she has it, am I going to say anything else? Am I going to lie? (*Silence. Rajadhyaksha laughs. Pradnya too.*) See how confident you are about my dishonesty! . . . I did not give the consent in writing because when she rang up . . . (*The phone rings. Rajadhyaksha gets up, still talking. Light on Pradnya fades out as he walks towards the phone and fades in on Uttara in B.*) . . . I didn't feel the necessity. Never thought there would be such a furore, such mudslinging . . . Hello!

UTTARA. Rajadhyaksha?

RAJA. Uttara?

UTTARA. How did you know?

RAJA. How? (*Trying to remain calm.*) Your voice—

UTTARA. What's wrong with yours?

RAJA. Age.

UTTARA. I called because—

RAJA. It's so long since I heard you last. Thirty years.

UTTARA. You see . . . I . . .

RAJA. I'm so glad.

UTTARA. I meant to write, but—

RAJA. So you could drop your pride at last. For years I went on writing to you and for years you never wrote back! Aren't we old enough to forget the past?

UTTARA (*suddenly*). I'm publishing a book!

RAJA (*happy*). Good. Oh, good!

UTTARA. So I thought I should . . .

RAJA. Lovely. Is it a novel or—

UTTARA. No, not a novel.

RAJA. I see! I told you so often—remember?—you should write, you see life more closely than I do. You're more intense. Why didn't you just get up and come here? It's thirty years now. Things have changed.

UTTARA. It's not a novel.

RAJA. Poems? Essays?

UTTARA. Letters.

RAJA. Why don't we forget the past, Uttara?

UTTARA. Who does the cooking?

RAJA. There's a bai. And I have a boy called Baban. He stays here with me. And the driver's there.

UTTARA. Is your astronomy still on?

RAJA. Oh yes! My stars haven't forsaken me. Every night they rise for me. Ever so loyally.

UTTARA. Vasanti said you write in some journal about the stars and planets.

RAJA. When did she start reading such stuff?

UTTARA. She met a girl who's doing some research on your work.

RAJA. Pradnya. She asked me before she went. Called on Vasanti. Vasanti still has the manuscript of one of my novels. Do you meet her?

UTTARA. Yes. Who else does she have?

RAJA. And you?

UTTARA (*laughs*). Well, I have my arthritis, my blood pressure—

RAJA. Asthma?

UTTARA. Oh yes, asthma too! It follows me everywhere. Faithfully.

RAJA. I hope you're taking care.

UTTARA. Oh, let that be. It's long distance from Pune. Won't waste time. So you don't mind?

RAJA. How can I mind?

UTTARA. They are your letters. *I* only received them.

RAJA. You'll print them?

UTTARA. Why not?

RAJA. What will you get out of it?

UTTARA. Heard you're writing your autobiography.

RAJA. So?

UTTARA. People should know my side of the story too.

RAJA. You'll never change, Uttara. (*Pause.*) Give them to me. They'll come in handy for my book.

UTTARA. Have *you* changed then?

RAJA (*frustrated and angry*). Do as you like.

UTTARA. Well, I've asked you now. I wouldn't like people to say that I didn't go through with the formality of asking your permission.

RAJA. Why don't we meet?

UTTARA. Take care.

Both wait for the other to hang up. Then put down the receivers together. Raja-dhyaksha walks towards Pradnya, talking. Light on Uttara fades out and fades in on Pradnya and Rajadhyaksha.

RAJA. . . . She wanted to meet me. I could feel that. But she didn't want to say it. There was a tremor in her voice. Age has set in on her. She's had to face a lot too. I said: Come, let's meet—what was the point anyway? Yet . . . So, finally, I told her to do as she liked.

PRADNYA. But that, surely, was not consent.

RAJA. She published the letters, people gorged on our lives. What did she get out of it? She had so much else to tell. She was a dancer in those days! Gave it up when we married. Went on to socialism with my socialist friends. Anyway, it doesn't matter any more. Aren't you going home? And where's your tea?

PRADNYA. I'll get it in a minute.

RAJA. Relax. Baban will make some.

PRADNYA. God! His tea! How can you even think of drinking that stuff?

RAJA. Don't hang around for too long. That chappy of yours will curse me if you're late.

PRADNYA. Who? Pamya?

RAJA. Prince Charming!

PRADNYA. We aren't meeting today.

RAJA. Really? Had a fight or something?

PRADNYA. Yeah.

RAJA. What else can you do anyway? You've been picking fights all day with me.

PRADNYA (*querulous*). When did I ever fight with you?

RAJA. All through the day you've been telling me I'm a bad, mediocre writer.

PRADNYA. Sorry.

RAJA. Now, I don't mind, because it's true—a little of it anyway.

PRADNYA. I didn't pick a fight with Pramod. He did.

RAJA. Serious? Fighting can be great fun when you're in love, but then you should never stretch it beyond a—

PRADNYA. He never has the guts to hold on. I do.

RAJA. You are a marvellous idiot in any case.

PRADNYA. Now even he has learnt to talk like this from you. Hardly met you once and he's so impressed and all that. All because you ignored me and talked to him. That flattered him and he decided he likes you.

RAJA. But I liked him. That hulk of yours.

PRADNYA. Has a flat nose. And is getting fatter by the moment. God, how he eats! It's obscene!

RAJA. Go, patch up with him. You'll be sorry all your life if he gets out of your clutches.

PRADNYA. How dare he get out! Know what he'll do? He'll smoulder, and then he'll eat and eat and eat for two days and then he'll come to me. On his knees

RAJA. Such a fascinating ego! Sitting pretty on your nose. And are your eyes a little red?

PRADNYA. How very imaginative! Do you or don't you want tea? I'm making some for myself.

RAJA. OK. And don't you cry in the kitchen.

Pradnya goes off to the kitchen in a huff, leaving Rajadhyaksha restless. Finally he gets up, takes a peep at Pradnya, goes to the phone stealthily and dials. Light on B. Phone rings. Vasanti (50) enters and picks it up.

VASANTI. Hullo!

RAJA. Uttara?

VASANTI. No, it's Vasanti. Who's—

RAJA. Sorry.

VASANTI. Anantrao?

RAJA. No, I mean . . . I wanted to speak to Uttara.

VASANTI. Tai's in bed. I'll wake her up.

RAJA. In bed? At this hour? Why, is there . . .

VASANTI. She's a little unwell.

RAJA. Has the doctor . . .

VASANTI. He came. There's nothing to worry about. It's just ordinary fever. (*Pause.*)

RAJA. OK

VASANTI. Is there any message?

RAJA. No, no. I just wanted to tell her not to be upset. A lot's being written about the book, so . . .

VASANTI. She's not upset.

RAJA. The Foreword is very good. Very dignified.

VASANTI. I'll tell her that. (*Pause.*)

RAJA. How are you?

VASANTI. I'm all right.

RAJA. What's all right?

VASANTI. All right! What else?

RAJA. This is rather unexpected, isn't it? Talking to you after so long.

VASANTI. Thirty years!

RAJA. You still remember!

VASANTI. I didn't make any particular effort to forget. It's not that significant.

RAJA. You didn't even let me justify

VASANTI. I didn't want you to. I didn't want any justification from you and I wasn't going to give you any. I'll hang up.

RAJA. Look after Uttara. (*Pause.*)

VASANTI. She doesn't like my coming here much.

RAJA. Hmm.

VASANTI. She doesn't like Salim.

RAJA. I'll hang up.

VASANTI. Won't you ask who's Salim?

RAJA. That painter.

VASANTI. And my lover. Of now. We're living together. In puritan Pune.

RAJA. Shocking people has always been your hobby.

VASANTI. Tai wants me to leave him. I listened to her once. She wanted me to leave you—I did. Now I'm not that obedient, OK. (*Hangs up. Light on Rajadhyaksha fades out. Vasanti in light in B. Uttara enters.*) Why did you get up? Lie down.

UTTARA. Who was it? (*Pause.*)

VASANTI (*trying to gauge Uttara's reaction*). Anantrao.

UTTARA (*unruffled*). Hm.

VASANTI. You don't look surprised. (*Pause.*) Does he ring often?

UTTARA. Second time in all these years. Oh no, this leg!

VASANTI. Let me massage it. (*She massages Uttara's leg.*)

UTTARA. Thought he was telling you something about the book.

VASANTI. The newspapers are in great glee over it.

UTTARA. Vasu, why don't you dye your hair now? It's more white than black.

VASANTI. Oh, never mind. I don't even dance any more.

UTTARA. I shouldn't have published those letters.

VASANTI. It's too late now.

UTTARA. But for his phone call that day, it wouldn't have ever entered my mind to publish them.

VASANTI. People have got good fodder to chew on. A repeat performance when his autobiography comes.

UTTARA. Oh, he'll not write much. (*Laughs*.) Some bland, vague stuff. Don't you know him? Readers will get nothing. And the truth, never! That has always been his style.

VASANTI. Then why did you have to publish his letters?

UTTARA. He thought I'd use them. He had the nerve to think that. That made me mad. Thought let people know the truth. They have such horrible misconceptions about you and me.

VASANTI. Will they know the truth from your book?

UTTARA. They are all his letters.

VASANTI. That's it, only his. Where are the letters you wrote to him? (*Pause*.)

Uttara is a little restless.

UTTARA. I didn't write to him much. I was never good at letter-writing. You know that. That's enough, Vasu. Don't tire yourself.

VASANTI. Then don't call him vague.

UTTARA. Vasu, you still feel so deeply about him, don't you?

VASANTI. Maybe the truth is on your side. But he too should have the right to state his case. He shouldn't be made to put up with any injustice.

UTTARA (*after a moment's pause*). You talk as if you left him only to burden me with a favour. I'll have to live with this gratitude for ever now.

VASANTI. I felt guilty. You were his wife.

UTTARA (*smiles*). Never.

VASANTI. Believe me, Tai. I wasn't very happy to.

UTTARA. Nonsense. That's not true. There have been many men who have come into your life and gone. I was just an excuse for you. I am sure, in a year or two, you would have walked out on him in any case.

VASANTI. You can be so cruel and yet laugh about it. (*Pause.*) He was the first man in my life. (*Pause.*)

UTTARA. Enough is enough, Vasanti—now get married to Salim. Let Dilip have a father, a home.

VASANTI. Oh yeah? Father and son, nearly the same age!

UTTARA. Even Dilip should be getting married now. Tell him. He's almost thirty.

VASANTI. As if he listens to me! Every time I talk to him it's the same answer: Not yet!

UTTARA. I wish Devadatta had lived. That child would have had a father, then.

VASANTI. In a sense, Dilip does belong to Devadatta. (*Lost.*) I used to feel so secure when I was with him.

UTTARA. He did have that something in him. And he had to die young. And how his name spelt insomnia to Anant! These writers just cannot stand the existence of each other. Pass that cushion to me. Why don't you stay for dinner? Salim's not back yet.

VASANTI. Oh no. If he gets home suddenly, he won't like it at all.

UTTARA. You're still scared of him?

VASANTI (*putting on*). Oh! You don't know his temper. He must have me around all the time. Dilip keeps calling me to Assam, but if I go, Salim will follow me all the way there! (*Uttara stares at her.*) Why do you stare?

UTTARA. No, nothing.

VASANTI. You think it's all a lie.

UTTARA. Did I say that, Vasu? Don't— (*Pause.*)

VASANTI. People think we won't last long, only because Salim's younger than me. Anantrao must have been shocked when I told him.

UTTARA. What did he say?

VASANTI. He didn't say anything, I was just thinking . . . But he did seem upset about the book. How did he know you were going to publish those letters?

UTTARA. News must have travelled. Dandekar might have talked. What publisher will dare upset him?

VASANTI. He must have been furious.

UTTARA. He phoned at midnight. I was awake reading. Wondered who it could be at that hour. (*The phone rings. Uttara goes to it. Light only on Uttara as she speaks into the phone and on Rajadhyaksha in A.*) I don't sleep too well these days, so I stay up with some book. Hullo . . .

RAJA. Uttara?

UTTARA. Yes?

RAJA. Uttara? (*Pause.*) Know me? (*Pause.*)

UTTARA. Rajadhyaksha?

RAJA. Know my voice? (*Pause.*)

UTTARA. One hears it on the radio, TV. (*Pause.*)

RAJA. What's wrong with your voice?

UTTARA (*laughs*). Age!

RAJA. How are you, Uttara?

UTTARA. OK.

RAJA. I knew your voice even after so many years. Thirty. (*Pause.*) Heard about your book.

UTTARA (*after a moment or two*). Who told you?

RAJA. Is it true?

UTTARA. Why do you ask?

RAJA. Give me those letters. I'm writing my autobiography. I want to do full justice to you. (*Pause.*)

UTTARA. You have my letters. Use them. (*Pause.*)

RAJA. All right. Take care of yourself.

UTTARA. Who does the cooking?

RAJA. There's a bai. And a boy called Baban. He stays here with me. And the driver's there.

UTTARA. Is your astronomy still on?

RAJA. Yes, of course. My stars still rise for me. Ever so loyally. (*Pause.*) Why don't you come here, Uttara ? It's been ages now.

UTTARA. Heard you write articles for some journal. How did you turn to that? Vasanti was telling me, she met a girl who's doing some research on your work.

RAJA. Pradnya. She asked me before she went to see Vasanti. Vasanti still has the manuscript of one of my novels. You meet her?

UTTARA. Very often. She says: Who else do I have but her? I say I have my arthritis, my blood pressure . . . and my faithful asthma. Vasanti really looks after me.

RAJA. Is your decision final, Uttara?

UTTARA. It wasn't until now. Till you called I had thought I won't publish them.

RAJA. You should have at least asked me, as a formality.

UTTARA. Would you have given me the permission? And are you going to stick to all these formalities when you write your book?

RAJA. My book is an AUTOBIOGRAPHY! (*Pause. In a calmer voice.*) Give it a thought again. (*Pause.*) Take care. Let me know if you need anything. I'll just leave everything and come.

UTTARA. Thank you. I don't think you'll have to. Take care. I'll hang up. (*Both wait for the other to hang up. Then put down the receivers together. Uttara walks to Vasanti. Light now on Vasanti.*) Weren't you surprised when he called on his own?

RAJA. I was. (*Pause.*) Hear he's really old now. He must have needed some excuse to get in touch.

UTTARA. He's not the type. Not the type at all. He would want people to come to him. And then wait for him. For days and days. Wouldn't even talk to them till their pride, their dignity was totally crushed. He's not someone who'll ring up on some pretext.

RAJA. You're still so bitter. He must have changed now. Don't people mellow with age?

UTTARA. He kept asking me to see him. I almost gave in for a moment. He was afraid.

RAJA. And were you happy that he was afraid?

UTTARA. No. Really it wasn't good . . . I saw the man change in front of my eyes! A pure lyric poet, gave himself totally to the freedom movement, went to jail, became so corrupt after Independence. Wanted suddenly to grab the price for all he did, like all Gandhians. No one could rise above that corruption, not even the artists.

RAJA. Priorities change as one grows up.

UTTARA. Hollow things gained importance for him. And you know what he lost in the bargain? His sensitivity. Small, little, sweet but valuable things. He lost them. He was exposed so badly in the Emergency. It was sad. Such a sensitive, tender man, so like a child. Went on to become so callous

VASANTI (*looking at Uttara getting emotional*). It's been a long time, Tai. Why don't you meet?

UTTARA. He wanted to come. I said: Don't.

RAJA. And you talk about his ego.

UTTARA. All we can get out of it is torment. And he was only interested in his letters. That was what really upset me. He knows me, Vasu, so what if we are separated?

RAJA. Things could be clearer if you met.

UTTARA. Not at all. He would pressurize me. Very, very subtly. Without my knowing it.

RAJA. You shouldn't let him.

UTTARA. I wasn't sure of myself.

RAJA. Is that you talking, Tai? You've been so firm, like steel all your life.

UTTARA. I'm getting old now. I can't resist much. It's best to avoid him. And he knows my weaknesses. (*Tired.*) I'm exhausted now, all worn out. He shouldn't see me like this.

VASANTI (*smiles*). He would look after you.

UTTARA. That he would. Certainly. He would do that and I would be won over. All over again. How he cares for the sick, Vasu! When I couldn't sleep for my asthma, he would be up with me all night—now hot water, now tea— and so gladly . . . (*Controls herself firmly.*)

VASANTI. Easy, Tai, I'll get you some tea.

Vasanti exits. Fade out on B, fade in on A. Rajadhyaksha in his chair. Pradnya brings in the tea.

PRADNYA. How's the tea?

RAJA. Not enough sugar.

PRADNYA. It's enough. You shouldn't take too much sugar now.

RAJA. Don't be a tyrant. You do this to him too? He'll bolt.

PRADNYA. He dare not.

RAJA. Why not? He'll get a hundred girls like you.

PRADNYA. Like hell! Hides under a table when he sees a girl.

RAJA. Get married, quick! I'll give you away in marriage. At my age, one feels one has missed all these sweet little things in life.

PRADNYA. My mother will be most pleased. After father's death, she finds everything a pain.

RAJA. Where did you meet this . . . Mr Pamya?

PRADNYA. Know how much I had to lead him on? For six long months. I was literally chasing him. And then, one morning, he comes to me and says— know what he says?—he says, 'Hullo!' Once I saw him at the bus stop. I crashed in there, braked almost on his toes and asked, 'Want a lift?' He almost swooned.

RAJA. He can't have thought you a very nice girl at all!

PRADNYA. Yeah! So you know what I did? For a long time I wore only sarees and all, and talked very little and blushed and all, and then told him, 'See how you've changed me!' And then, after that, he began to thaw. I mean, he almost melted. Started sending me notes: 'You are my Kindly Light'; 'You are the sacred flower of God's own abode' et cetera, et cetera . . . Oh, you should have seen him, that six-footer giant, your 'hulk', writing such syrupy notes.

RAJA. So maybe he's read my novels after all.

PRADNYA. Then I had to do it. I mean I just had to. One day I sat before him and smoked. That did the trick, made him normal. Ah, falling in love is such a waste of time!

RAJA. You tell ME that! There was a time when I'd rocked all Maharashtra with my celebrated affair. People still talk about it nostalgically.

PRADNYA. You've made that portion so insipid, so dead in your book. No heat, no blood . . .

RAJA. You mean, no warmth, no blood.

PRADNYA. It's frozen.

RAJA. Your diction's all wrong, darling.

PRADNYA. You should rewrite that portion, in fact.

RAJA. I wanted to treat it with a lot of restraint.

PRADNYA. Restraint is not concealment.

RAJA. I didn't intend to conceal—but—

PRADNYA. Whatever maybe your intention. But the reader is bound to feel: Something is being withheld from me, I'm being cheated. Why do you want to tell me even this? He's bound to feel that.

RAJA. Why should the reader lap up my life? What respect can he have for my personal anguish?

PRADNYA. He will have respect for your anguish if you respect it yourself in the first place. Depends on how you write it.

RAJA. Yeah, go on, teach me how to write now.

PRADNYA. I'm talking about the reader.

RAJA. Let the reader go to hell.

PRADNYA. Don't write then.

RAJA. I will. Let's see who can stop me.

PRADNYA. Who's bothering to stop you?

RAJA. So?

PRADNYA. You are not proving anything by being childish.

RAJA. I'm NOT proving anything.

PRADNYA (*trying not to laugh*). But you'll have to.

RAJA. I won't. What do you say to that?

PRADNYA. You've made a statement about restraint in writing: 'The power, the strength in restrained writing is nowhere to be found in hysterical expression. But restraint is not stingy expression or a cover for one's limitations.'

RAJA (*firmly*). I have not said this anywhere.

PRADNYA (*firmly*). You have. You have said this in Chapter 3 of your book of critical essays, *Sahitya Vichar*, with reference to Devadatta's poems. That's your only article on Devadatta. Your 'unfavourite' contemporary.

RAJA. Another boomerang. You love to do this.

PRADNYA. I am a research student.

RAJA. You have no kindness, no compassion. You're not even civil. Get out of here.

PRADNYA (*trying not to laugh*). Sure?

RAJA. Oh sure! What do you think—?

PRADNYA. Won't call me up again?

RAJA. God! Haven't I spoilt you? (*Pause.*) There was a time when once a relationship was over, it was over for good. Snapped. And now I keep phoning you, asking you to come. Even when you're so callous about me.

PRADNYA (*a little stunned. After a moment*). I'll give up the research, OK?

RAJA. You're an idiot.

PRADNYA. I'll take up some other subject.

RAJA. Idiot. You think you'll get something as easy as this? (*Laughs.*)

PRADNYA. Now, who's doing the—?

RAJA. You will not change your subject.

PRADNYA. But you're so touchy about every little thing. In my thesis, I'll write so many bad things about you. You'll banish me from your life, then! Won't even see my face!

RAJA. I will, I will, OK? Write what you want. Who does even that for us now?

PRADNYA. You're saying this now. What if you change? And whatever happens, at any cost, I don't want to lose you as a friend.

RAJA. Why? You must have friends by the dozen.

PRADNYA. I haven't.

RAJA. Pamya?

PRADNYA. Oh Pamya! He's the boyfriend! You know, I use your name a lot to make him jealous!

RAJA. Oh God!

PRADNYA. How he gets mad! Then I tell him he doesn't understand me as much as you do. Then he says I flirt with you!

RAJA. Oh no! I don't understand you all that well. Not at all, in fact.

PRADNYA. Then why do you keep calling me?

RAJA. I feel good with you around. Not because I understand you. Maybe I wouldn't feel so good if I did. And then you want to be with someone because you feel good that way. Not because you understand or don't understand that person.

PRADNYA. Don't you ever feel like probing into your relationships? Analysing them?

RAJA. Analysis means delving into complexities, getting entangled in them, it means agony!

PRADNYA. And, just imagine, you're known as the writer 'who plumbs the depths of human relationships'!

RAJA. Like writers, like critics. Once I used to believe that myself. And critics need some label to tag on to you. I must have given them the idea myself and they just pounced on it.

PRADNYA. I never accepted that label.

RAJA. Your generation will not. When I look back now, I feel differently. Of an iceberg you can at least see the tip. Of relationships, you don't even see that much.

PRADNYA. Can I ask you something?

RAJA. Students need not observe such formalities

PRADNYA. When you say you don't understand relationships, you mean relationships in life or relationships the characters have in your literature?

RAJA. Both. Or, rather, the relationships in my literature are attempts to understand the relationships in my life. Relationships I couldn't figure out.

PRADNYA. Isn't that fantasizing?

RAJA. At times, yes, when they get mixed up.

PRADNYA. Then where's the authenticity? And people like to think—

RAJA. These relationships—they are valid only in the autonomous world of art—they have nothing to do with the external world—

PRADNYA. —that this character is this person, that is, that or this character's realistic, that—

RAJA. Why do you look for our characters in the external world?

PRADNYA. Because you start there. Some novels are termed autobiographical!

RAJA (*smiling*). Oh, I see!

PRADNYA. In such novels, how much is reality, how much fantasy, how much their blend and how much absolute lies? And if we are not supposed to look for characters in the outside world, why should we call the novel autobiographical? And if we are not supposed to call it autobiographical, why are events in it taken from real life?

RAJA. What are you trying to . . .

PRADNYA. Give me an example . . .

RAJA. You want me to talk about my novel! Say that!

PRADNYA (*laughs*). *The Misty Path*. Must have been a very modem title in those days.

RAJA. Even the novel was considered to be modern then! Was a great success. 'Success, in the long run, is the praise showered on you by your contemporaries. Even a Nobel Prize, if given posthumously, is useless in the ultimate analysis.' This definition is not mine. It is Devadatta's, whom your new generation has rediscovered recently.

PRADNYA. You're talking like a real clever boy today. You deserve a prize!

RAJA. Tea . . .

PRADNYA. No, no . . .

RAJA. . . . with lots of . . .

PRADNYA. . . . not tea . . .

RAJA. . . . sugar . . .

PRADNYA. . . . no way. You'll stay awake all night.

RAJA. That's mean.

PRADNYA. You are trying to get out of talking about the *Misty Path*. I know you, mister!

RAJA. You do take the cake for self-confidence, miss!

PRADNYA. I saw the old newspaper clippings. What an uproar!

RAJA. That was quite unexpected. Even for me.

PRADNYA. And the similarity critics found between your life and the novel was the similarity in names! In real life it was—

RAJA. Uttara and Vasanti. In the novel it was Urmila and Vasudha. And Anand for your Anant.

RAJA. Charudatta for Devadatta—

PRADNYA. Was the criticism in those days that juvenile?

RAJA. Why? Weren't my names also that? I had taken enough care to remind the readers of real people all the time.

PRADNYA. Now see? In the autobiography, you hide everything under the name of restraint, and in the novel—

RAJA. Listen! On one level, Urmila and Vasudha are Uttara and Vasanti, but on another, they aren't. That is only an attempt to understand them both.

PRADNYA. One doesn't feel that. After reading the novel, one feels: Poor, poor hero! How he's caught between these two women, and a silly rival like Charudatta! He becomes so poor—poor that all his poor-poorness becomes phoney. How can anybody get that poor-poor? I think that's where your novel fails.

RAJA. Perhaps! But I did try to rise above personal sentiments and look at our relationships objectively, as an outsider. My only mistake was, I think, that I painted events just as they happened, in reality. Made only minor changes. Like, I made Vasanti a painter instead of a dancer, which is what she really is.

PRADNYA. Devadatta-Charudatta in the novel is shown to be a puny man, a mediocre writer full of malice.

RAJA. And he was the type, I think

PRADNYA. Shall we suppose, then, that it is the limitation of your generation's perception?

RAJA. Died premature. If he had lived, maybe

PRADNYA. There is a renewed interest in him now. Joglekar has written three articles on him. Read those?

RAJA. Joglekar is free to say anything.

PRADNYA. Hmm. Many others have started feeling the same. He was ahead of . . .

RAJA. . . . But that doesn't mean . . .

PRADNYA. . . . much ahead of his times . . .

RAJA. . . . that I should feel the same. And time . . .

PRADNYA. His contemporaries neglected him . . .

RAJA. Now, that's not true. So often he was invited to various committees, seminars, conferences. But the spiteful fellow preferred to stay away. (*Pause.*)

PRADNYA. I think we're talking about two different things. (*Pause.*) How did you feel when Vasanti went to live with him?

RAJA. It was sad, humiliating. She left me, I could take that. But for whom? Some pauper of a writer without any talent. Why do you stare at me like that?

PRADNYA. There are no photographs of him that I could find.

RAJA. He was quite OK to look at. But ridden with diseases. Alcohol.

PRADNYA. And?

RAJA. Why do you make me talk about him?

PRADNYA. Because one doesn't find this in your autobiography.

RAJA. I get a little scared of you at times

PRADNYA (*smiles*). I'm not going to write about this or about you anywhere.

RAJA. You know how small I am. And yet you come. We may start despising each other.

PRADNYA. Who else do I have to go to? It's unbearable to sit at home. Baba's been dead for over fifteen years but my mother refuses to get out of it. He was brilliant. And handsome!

RAJA. Death is so gentle to the dead. The ones left behind have to face hell. Even this Devadatta died with all the tensions between us intact. Leaving me to bear that pain alone till I pop off.

PRADNYA. But were there really any tensions from his side? He's said such good things about you in one of his letters. In his last illness

RAJA (*with real concern*). He was in such pain! He'd become an invalid. A stubborn, obstinate fellow—a man of steel. Somewhere, deep within, I had great admiration for him. I didn't want him to break. I felt that strongly. Even at the end.

PRADNYA. He has written about it. What are the lines now? Yes . . . 'Mr Rajadhyaksha, like an elder brother, visits me often. I have seen the largeness of his heart. I've known how tender his feelings are. It has strengthened my love for him. I wouldn't have been able to face this illness without the help he has given me, economically, psychologically, spiritually!'

RAJA (*embarrassed*). So what? The fellow was a bit too emotional anyway.

PRADNYA. About your writing—

RAJA (*smiling*). Never said a word. Not a word. I wanted him to say good things about my writing. But he didn't do that even when he was dying. That was all right too. (*Pause.*) Vasanti went to him. He gave her a baby without any thought and went on to die. Lived a pauper and made her addicted to that kind of living . . . And what did Vasanti get out of all her adventures? Drilled as a C-grade dancer for a while and now runs 'dancing classes' for schoolgirls! And a new boyfriend every two–three years . . . the poor child must be going crazy with all the men in her life.

PRADNYA. But in the novel—

RAJA. Reality was too hard for me.

PRADNYA. So? In the novel, Vasanti, that is Vasudha, carries the hero's child. But Vasudha is left desolate and lonely when the hero is thrown into prison for participating in the freedom movement. In her helplessness, she turns to Charudatta who, in a sentimental moment of magnanimity, agrees to be the child's father.

RAJA. All this is what you call my mushy idealism. Hero in jail, heroine in distress, a generous-hearted rival who forgets everything magnanimously.

PRADNYA. Exactly. Everything glorified, simplified . . .

RAJA (*sentimental*). Tell you something? (*Pause. Then in a husky voice.*) I wanted that to be true in real life. I was so fond of babies. (*Clears his throat.*)

PRADNYA. He lives in Assam now.

RAJA. Who?

PRADNYA. Dilip. Remember, I went to get that manuscript from Vasanti? That Salim was ragging her at that time. Seems Dilip hasn't written her a word in the last eight years. Salim was being so cruel!

RAJA. What else can the poor boy do? That Salim is thirty-five and he is thirty. She's thrown everything to the winds. I'm worried for the boy. And I haven't even seen him. That I should care for Devadatta's child is another irony! But now I can't bear to see lives being wasted away like that. We did that to our lives, that was bad enough. And that is why I'm worried about you, you idiot.

PRADNYA. One doesn't decide to ruin one's life. It happens.

RAJA. Uttara used to say: You deliberately ruined our lives. Hers and Vasanti's. She could never accept the fact that things 'happened'. Otherwise, how could a quiet, dignified Uttara become a hysteric when she saw things getting out of her control? It was baffling. Was that the real Uttara? Or the other one?

Rajadhyaksha walks into C as he speaks the last lines. Fade out. As lights fade in, Rajadhyaksha and Uttara are in C.

UTTARA. What did you gain, ruining our lives? Tell me.

RAJA. I don't know myself.

UTTARA. Tell me . . . tell me . . .

RAJA. Quiet, Uttara . . .

UTTARA. A great writer, aren't you? Master of my life! And now you want to be the master of my sister's life, too.

RAJA. I'm ashamed of what happened, Uttara.

UTTARA. She came to this house with such trust! Younger than you by twenty-five years! Where's all your morality and idealism vanished now?

RAJA. Uttara—please!

UTTARA. Could be our daughter! We had no children. And when she came, I was so happy, so relieved to think that she could be our own daughter. But without the least compunction you have destroyed us both. Where will she go now?

RAJA. Why should she go anywhere?

UTTARA. Have you no shame at all? Vasanti will not stay here.

RAJA. I am just as responsible as she is in all that happened.

UTTARA. Don't you dare have anything to do with her. I'll burn myself alive in front of your eyes.

RAJA. I'll not desert her.

UTTARA. What did you see in her? Beauty? Youth? To seduce—

RAJA. Don't use those ugly words. You were keen to bring her into the house when I was saying no. When she came, you ill-treated her.

UTTARA. I only asked her to help around the house. Don't I do the chores myself? What's wrong if—

RAJA. You constantly tried to find fault with her. Because you were afraid, weren't you? Or jealous? . . . I knew it . . . she was lonely in this house.

UTTARA. You want to destroy me. Because I couldn't bear your child.

RAJA. I told you. Told you often: Let's adopt some orphan child.

UTTARA. Kill me! Kill me! That will make you happy.

As Uttara cries, lights fade out. Fade in on A: Rajadhyaksha and Pradnya.

RAJA. She was hysterical. The grief of childlessness buried deep inside her suddenly burst out. It had erupted sometimes even before that. And then it was hell—she didn't care who she was talking to, what she was saying.

PRADNYA. In the novel Uttara-Urmila is extremely high strung, the opposite of Vasudha. How did Uttara-bai react when she heard?

RAJA. I can't bear to imagine the scene between those two! I didn't even see Vasanti after that fight with Uttara. She left the house that same night. (*Pause.*) Uttara too.

PRADNYA. You never met Vasanti again?

RAJA. When I went to see Devadatta in his illness, she was always around, but never came near me. Only the shuffle of her feet, the clinking of her bangles. I think she didn't have enough confidence—in herself. She was madly in love with me.

PRADNYA. So that terrible scene between Urmila and Vasudha—it's all imagination?

RAJA. Imagination. But I didn't have to try too hard. It must've been exactly like that, word by word. I'm positive. I still don't know how Uttara got to know about us but I'm sure Vasanti told her. She was hardly twenty, younger than Uttara by twenty years. And she was so unexposed, naive, lonely . . . the tension of a secret affair must have been too much for her. Remember how it happens in the novel? It's a rude shock to Urmila.

PRADNYA. But if Urmila had some faint suspicion, she would have been more subtle, more real as a character. What woman will be so . . . so unwary? Now it's all so silly. Vasudha is cleaning the closet, saying some meaningless things, and suddenly: 'Tai, I want to tell you something.'

VASUDHA. Urmila-tai—

URMILA. Not again! Must you talk so much? I've almost got a headache.

VASUDHA. I must talk to you.

URMILA. OK, then. I can't stop you.

VASUDHA. I . . . I . . .

URMILA. What is it? (*Pause.*)

VASUDHA. Anandrao and I . . . (*Pause.*) . . . have fallen in love.

URMILA (*stands up*). What? (*Vasudha—muffled sobs*). What did you say? (*Vasudha sobs.*) Are you in your senses? (*Grabs Vasudha's hair.*) What . . . (*Vasudha sobs uncontrollably.*) Since when has this been going on? Vasu? Vasu—

VASUDHA. Last year . . . When you went to the camp for two weeks.

URMILA. You did this to your own sister?

VASUDHA. Tai, I was so lonely . . . We didn't realize what happened—we—he made me feel so secure.

URMILA. You cast some dirty spell on him, and how brazenly you talk about it. Shameless! How far have you gone? (*Vasudha cries.*) How close are you? (*Vasudha cries.*) Hm. (*Vasudha cannot control her sobs.*) I hope you haven't done something foolish. (*Shocked, she touches Vasudha's stomach.*) Tell me, tell me. (*Vasudha is silent. Urmila sighs.*) My fate! (*Pause.*) Get out. Get out of here. This moment. Or I'll set you on fire.

VASUDHA. Where can I go, Tai?

URMILA. Anywhere. What's that to someone like you? Oh God! Thank God that Aai–Baba are not alive to see all this. Get out.

VASUDHA. I cannot live without Anandrao.

URMILA. He's sitting in jail, gazing at his stars. God knows when he'll come home. You get going.

VASUDHA. Let me meet him . . . just once! For the last time!

URMILA. Are you going? Or shall I burm myself? (*Lights a match.*) Vasudha!

VASUDHA (*scared*). Don't, Tai, oh don't! I'll go.

Vasudha leaves. Urmila drops the match and weeps. Then comes into B, weeps, Vasanti near her. Lights in C fade out and fade in on B.

VASANTI. Uttara-tai

UTTARA. Sorry, Vasu.

VASANTI. You'll be ill again.

UTTARA. It's his phone call. It's upset me. He says he wants to meet me.

VASANTI. You must meet him, Tai. All misunderstandings—

UTTARA. There ARE no misunderstandings, Vasu, because there's no love. You just happened to be the cause.

VASANTI. Who knows!

UTTARA. It could've been any other girl in your place.

VASANTI. Why? Because he could never be in love with me?

UTTARA. It's not that.

VASANTI. It is.

UTTARA. Vasu—

VASANTI. For the last thirty years you've been trying to tell me this. That there was nothing in me for him to love.

UTTARA. No, Vasanti—

VASANTI. Didn't you ever see anything worthwhile in me?

UTTARA. You still get so worked up. (*Pause.*) We never talked about this before, we had lost touch for so long, but I'll tell you something now, had thought of telling you long ago. I talked to him the night you told me about it. I said: I'll go, you live with Vasu. (*Pause.*) But he wouldn't listen. He wanted to possess us both. And while we were talking, you just packed and then, without a word, left us to go to Devadatta. By then, for me, it was all over in that house anyway. I left too, that same night.

VASANTI. I'll never know what you said to each other.

UTTARA. I still remember every word of it. (*Dark. Light on C fades in. Uttara walks from B to C, talking. In the following scene, Uttara talks sadly, not in anger.*) I asked him: Why did you do this? Why this act of indiscretion?

RAJA (*has entered in C*). Things happen, Uttara.

UTTARA. God! What a mess! No one's going to gain anything out of it.

RAJA. Don't make me feel more wretched now.

UTTARA. She came here with such trust! Younger than you by twenty-five years. How could you? With all your ideas of morality, your idealism?

RAJA. Uttara, please—

UTTARA. I was so happy, I thought: This is my child now.

RAJA. I won't abandon her. We'll send her somewhere. She can continue in college.

UTTARA. How can you even say this? She will not go anywhere. This will be her home now.

RAJA. You go to such extremes!

UTTARA. You are saying that to me! Don't you dare desert her. What did you see in her? Beauty? Youth?

RAJA. You brought her into the house when I was against it. When she came, you ill-treated her.

UTTARA. I only asked her to help around the house. Don't I do the chores? I wanted her to be occupied. (*Pause.*) Anyway, I won't stay here any more. It's best that way. (*From here on, starts walking into B.*) And, after all, what right did I have to stay there? I couldn't even give him a child.

C dark. Lights fade in on B.

VASANTI. Anyway, Tai, it doesn't matter any more. There's your side to it and there's his. I'll never know his.

UTTARA. Must you be so silly and obstinate? Even now?

VASANTI. I'm not obstinate, Tai. Maybe I'm not like that Vasudha of his novel— but silly, obstinate . . .

UTTARA. Then am I like that Urmila? It's all a hoax. You are the ever-suffering epitome of sacrifice. And me—a hysterical, fighting shrew. We are stuck with these images now. People will always believe him, a famous writer! That's one reason why I published his letters. Let people know the truth.

VASANTI. About that I am not so sure! Forget others, but are you very happy to tell the people the truth? Isn't it a torment? You lived alone all your life.

UTTARA. How he has made out that scene between us! Did I ever talk about fires and burnings?

VASANTI. That's a writer's imagination. How was he to know what really happened between us? (*Vasanti reads.*)

UTTARA. Such poor imagination! That man did not understand me and he did not understand you. Remember how it happened? You were reading calmly. Just like this. You were always so dangerously calm in those days. I kept staring at you. You turned round, looked me in the eye and said—

Lights change. Vasanti turns and looks Uttara in the eye.

VASANTI. Why do you look at me like that?

UTTARA. No, nothing.

VASANTI. Want to ask me something? Go ahead.

UTTARA. No, no.

VASANTI. You want to ask.

UTTARA. I don't want to ask you anything. (*Long pause.*)

VASANTI (*same calm voice*). It's true. (*Pause.*)

UTTARA. Don't be stupid.

VASANTI. Yes, Tai. It's true. (*Uttara restlessly takes up her knitting.*) Anantrao and I are very close.

UTTARA. I don't want to hear it.

VASANTI. But I want to tell you.

UTTARA. Why? . . . Why?

VASANTI. I want to be free of this. (*Pause.*)

UTTARA (*in a trembling voice*). You didn't think even once of what'll become of Tai?

VASANTI. We didn't have the time. And nothing will happen to you.

UTTARA. I had my fears, of course. But now you've bared it all. (*Suddenly, horrified.*) I hope nothing awful has happened to you. I mean

VASANTI. Don't panic. We have taken care.

UTTARA (*broken*). Vasu! (*Pause.*)

VASANTI. I'm leaving this house today. For good.

UTTARA. Where can you go? And it's not just you. Wait a while. Let me talk to him.

VASANTI. No. I want to go.

UTTARA. You stay here. I'll go.

VASANTI. You won't leave him. You have your nails dug tight into him. (*Pause.*) And it's over between him and me now. (*Pause.*)

UTTARA. Why did you do it?

VASANTI. Don't you understand? Really? . . . Tell me truly, don't you really know why this happened? (*Uttara nods to say no.*) I couldn't stand your over-weening ego. Your ego, which would not let you even look at anyone else. You're so immersed in your self—always, always revolving around your self. If you do lift your eye, it's only to look at someone with contempt. And you can cut people down to size, humiliate them, with such flair, with a smile on your face. You can cut a person to pieces without spilling a drop of blood. That's you.

UTTARA (*wounded*). When did I do that to you, my child?

VASANTI (*hurt*). Every bloody moment you show me how small I am, how I cannot rise to your level. If ever I have a dance show, you applaud me with all the guests, and then: 'You got this mudra wrong, baby, it's like this . . .' You say that right there, in front of them. And then you go on to show me how, with your graceful fingers! That would be enough to wipe out all the effect of my dance. You pat me in front of people, order me around in a tender voice . . . Oh, I'm fed up of being treated like an orphan.

UTTARA. This is horrible.

VASANTI. Aai–Baba always said marriage had changed you. Whenever you came home, you came like a visiting queen. Even to my poor Aai–Baba you were a queen, not their child. I didn't dare talk to you. (*Pause.*) And all that only because you had *him*. What was your worth—just that you had hooked a rich, clever, famous husband (*Pause.*) You have made me so small, so insignificant.

UTTARA. You'd come to Bombay from a small town. That was all. I didn't want you to look any different from me.

VASANTI. Was I ever in the running with you? For no reason you put on the airs of a winner, and then I made up my mind—I was determined to win Anantrao over from you. He was the source of all your airs, your strength after all.

UTTARA. Why didn't you tell me? . . . Why didn't you tell me when you knew I was wrong?

VASANTI. It all piled up. One humiliation on another . . . one insult on another.

UTTARA. Perhaps I was wrong. But him?

VASANTI. He had nothing but that in his eyes. From the first moment. (*Pause.*)

UTTARA. Vasu, you stay with him. I'll go away.

VASANTI. I won't stay here. I don't love him. (*Pause.*)

UTTARA (*quietly*). I won't stay here. I love him.

Light changes to original.

VASANTI. I thought I had won. I went to Devadatta, leaving you to reign over the ruins of that house. But you won again. You left the house too. That same night.

UTTARA. You had Devadatta. Who did I have?

VASANTI. Tai!

UTTARA. For two years after I came here, he wrote letters to me. (*Pause.*) Forget it, all that's past. Let's not fret over it, Vasu.

VASANTI. What a mess we've made of our lives!

UTTARA. Vasu, how did you get so close to him? Tell me. He's not the type at all. No harm telling me now.

VASANTI. He used to take me to the terrace at night. Because I was so alone. He always talked about the stars and showed me the stars—and one day, right there . . .

UTTARA (*laughing loudly*). You showed ME the stars all right. At noon (*Vasanti has tears in her eyes.*) What is it, Vasu ?

VASANTI. You laughed just now! You reminded me of my old Tai, before her marriage. My Tai who made my hair, who draped her new saree round me, who kissed me every morning when I went to school

UTTARA. And now we're together again. You and me. We meet. He doesn't have anyone . . . When he saw someone ill, he had the tenderness of a mother! The same tender hands. Could not believe it was the same man!

VASANTI. Remember Dr Sane? Who visited you in jail during the Emergency? Anantrao had sent him.

UTTARA. Must have been from his sense of guilt about managing to stay out. And he had been a freedom-fighter once. Faced lathis and gone to jail more than once. He had written in a letter: 'You are far above me—I couldn't give you anything.' He loved children. We were thinking of adopting some child, and then this . . . we are talking so much about him today.

Fade out on B. Light on A.

RAJA. Uttara, Uttara . . . we are talking so much about her today.

PRADNYA. You still think of her!

RAJA. Don't you? Of your . . . your Pramod must be waiting for you!

PRADNYA (*furious*). Pramod! Is he my boyfriend or yours?

RAJA. What's your problem? Can't I even mention his name? Something must be terribly wrong. What is it?

PRADNYA. Never mind. That's my problem.

RAJA. Is that so? And is it all right your digging into my personal life? . . . OK then. Get going. I've had enough.

PRADNYA. I'm sorry if I've hurt you.

RAJA. Hurt? Nonsense! You better go now.

PRADNYA. Don't behave like a spoilt child.

RAJA. It's time for my drink.

PRADNYA. So drink!

RAJA. You get going.

PRADNYA. Shall I get everything?

RAJA. Baban will.

PRADNYA. But can't I stay here when you drink?

RAJA. I get violent when I'm drunk.

PRADNYA. Come on!

RAJA. I may or may not. But I don't want you to stay here. You're almost driving me out! Where can I go? Don't ask me!

PRADNYA. I don't have anywhere to go. And Pramod is not meeting me today. Why today—tomorrow, the day after, for days we aren't meeting. (*Pause.*) We've had a real fight. (*Checks a sob.*)

RAJA (*worried*). That serious? (*Pradnya shakes her head.*) Tell him I've called him. (*She nods to say no.*) Won't say even that much to him? (*Pradnya is silent.*) Fine. Give me his address.

PRADNYA. You'll do no such thing. Why should you kneel before him?

RAJA. I've lost a lot in my life by not doing just that. I'll not make that mistake again, at this age. I shall kneel, even if it hurts.

PRADNYA. You do what you want for your own sake. I don't want you to stoop for me.

RAJA. This is dictatorship!

PRADNYA. I'll get your drink.

RAJA. Give me his address.

PRADNYA. Don't be stubborn.

RAJA. Give me his address.

PRADNYA. If you do this, I won't come here from tomorrow.

RAJA. Why tomorrow? Go now, right now and never come back.

> *Pradnya squats down, checking a sob.*

PRADNYA. How shall I explain? He'll insult you. We'll see.

RAJA. But why? You don't even know why we quarrelled. Tell me. (*Pause.*)

PRADNYA. He is against my carrying on with this research.

RAJA. Indeed! Is that all?

PRADNYA. Why do you laugh?

RAJA. You children! What a stupid thing to fight over. Just give it up.

PRADNYA. You think it very funny, don't you?

RAJA. Honest. Give it up. Edward VIII gave up his kingdom and you—

PRADNYA. It's not that simple. (*Pause.*) He doesn't really mind the research—

RAJA. What are you trying to say? Now this, now that.

PRADNYA. I can't really explain. (*Pause.*) What he objects to is my carrying out research on *your* works.

RAJA. Good heavens! Never thought there could be anyone so much against my writings.

PRADNYA. Who the hell is he to tell me what I should do and what I shouldn't?

RAJA. When did he read my books? You say he doesn't read the newspaper.

PRADNYA (*pause*). He's jealous. He feels you're more precious to me than him. He gets upset because I give all my time to you. He feels—

RAJA. Go on.

PRADNYA (*in a faint voice*). —That I'm getting involved with you. (*Pause.*)

RAJA. He IS rather stupid!

PRADNYA. It's pointless explaining to him

RAJA. But this is serious, Pradnya!

PRADNYA. I won't let him rule my life.

RAJA. Don't be rash

PRADNYA. Each day I'm going farther away from him. Because of his attitude. What does he think I am? Anyway, forget it.

Pradnya goes in. Rajadhyaksha is upset. Paces up and down. Goes into C without noticing it. C in light. A dark. Urmila and Vasudha in C.

URMILA. Isn't he looking lonely, Vasudha?

VASUDHA. His face looks all haggard. He's become so old, Urmila-tai!

URMILA. Could be that he is lonely.

VASUDHA. Isn't that funny? Wrote about lonely people all his life without knowing what loneliness was. And now when he knows what it is, he's stopped writing.

URMILA. That's exactly why!

VASUDHA. Why do such people bother writing at all?

URMILA. You can't use that word. 'Creative' is what they are called. They are into 'creating'!

VASUDHA. How terrible for us!

URMILA. They create a whole new universe!

VASUDHA. Who's asked them to? They have to create us, have to decide how we look, what we like and we have to feel happy, unhappy as they like— they take our entire lives into their hands! How mean of them!

URMILA. That's our destiny.

VASUDHA. But that destiny too is decided by them! He dictates to me on what page I should laugh, on what page I should cry. I'm not allowed to budge an inch on my own. He'll know what it's like when someone does that to him.

URMILA. But of course someone does that to them! Someone does decide their destiny without bothering to ask them. They too have their problems, their grievances.

VASUDHA. Oh, Tai! Must you always be so understanding? (*Giggles.*) How will he feel if he hears you talk like this? He's made you such a cold-hearted shrew.

URMILA. So I'll be that! Can't be helped.

VASUDHA. And me? Innocent as a babe, buried under suffering and injustice, for ever and ever—god! I want to rebel!

URMILA. You talk like him!

VASUDHA. And the silly gestures he's given me!

URMILA. You're supposed to be Vasanti, you see.

VASUDHA. But my gestures are not the same! She used to play with her pigtails—I wonder if she does that now, but it looked so cute! And what do I do! Chew my nails. Oh God!

URMILA. That is supposed to show that you are uneasy, shy . . .

VASUDHA. Same old tricks.

URMILA. But, then, he is a writer!

VASUDHA. Now don't you side with him all the time. He's ditched you in the novel. Better remember that.

URMILA. Readers don't mind if husbands ditch shrews. He should appear pitiable. That's all.

VASUDHA. I'm fed up with this decided destiny. Stupid joys and stupid sorrows! I want to live differently, more intensely . . . passionately! I want to get out of this prison!

URMILA. But writers ARE like that!

VASUDHA. He's so damned unfair to you. To Uttara too! Such a dignified lady, so self-respecting. Wonder how she felt when she read us.

URMILA. She must have hated me!

VASUDHA. We must confront him.

URMILA (*smiles*). Do that.

VASUDHA. Of course we must.

URMILA. SO do that. Who's stopping you?

VASUDHA. Sure? Don't blame me later.

URMILA. I won't . . . What will you tell him?

VASUDHA. I'll be frank and forthright. I'll say: 'You have no right to treat those two and us two like this. Spoils their name and ours too. And this confinement on top of it!'

URMILA. They'll be free in another few years, but we're immortal! Whether anyone reads his book or not.

VASUDHA. Then shall we do this? You do the talking.

URMILA. Is there any sense in this, Vasu? Is anything at all going to change? We'll remain just what we are, where we are.

VASUDHA. But at least he'll know where he went wrong.

URMILA. OK, if you wish.

Both approach Rajadhyaksha.

RAJA. Uttara! Vasanti!

URMILA. I'm not Uttara, I'm Urmila!

VASUDHA. I'm not Vasanti, I'm Vasudha!

RAJA. Who?

VASUDHA. Oh God!

URMILA. What's the matter? Don't you know us?

RAJA. Uttara, Vasanti . . .

VASUDHA. Will they ever set foot here now? Lucky ladies!

RAJA. Then why did you?

VASUDHA. Where else could we go?

RAJA. What can I do for you?

VASUDHA. You can't do anything. That's exactly what we came to tell you. You should've thought before.

URMILA. Vasu is a little upset, you see, because you made us so puny.

VASUDHA. Why did you do that?

URMILA. You should have let us behave like us. Your novel would have been so much better that way. You can't make your characters dance to your wish.

RAJA. The way I understood YOU.

URMILA. Or Uttara and Vasanti?

RAJA. Yes . . . I mean . . . they too

URMILA. You understood no one. Not them, not us.

VASUDHA. He didn't want to, in the first place. He just wanted to play 'I-am-suffering, I-am-suffering.' And all the suffering masked all so artistically. He never bothered about us, about our souls, our desires.

RAJA. You see, objectively . . .

URMILA. Not one bit. You styled us according to your likes and dislikes. I'm a shrew because you're cut up with Uttara. Charudatta's a bad writer because you're jealous of Devadatta. And you love Vasanti, so she's the innocent babe.

VASUDHA. Above all, poor helpless me, and so miserable—the helpless Anand, the hero! Why didn't you ever try to understand your self? There was no need for you to show that I turned to Charudatta only out of helplessness. Shall I tell you the truth? If I had a choice, I would have gone to him gladly. Happily. He was a genius.

URMILA. Enough, Vasu.

RAJA. Let her. It's quite important! (*Pause.*) What can I do for you now?

VASUDHA. I told you. It's too late.

RAJA. I . . . am quite aware that I've been unfair to you. Charudatta gave you Pradeep. I've shown in the novel that Pradeep is my child, Charudatta only brings him up. But, honestly, I wanted a son. Devadatta gave you a child and that shattered me. I know I'm wrong. I can see that. I've changed considerably in the last thirty years.

URMILA. Yes, it's quite commendable, but it's of no use to us any more. We have to remain what we are.

RAJA. Is it too late you think for things to change? Can't one correct even a single mistake? Has life just slipped by?

URMILA. But you will still escape, Rajadhyaksha. You are not doomed to immortality as we are.

RAJA. Nor are you. In a short time, everything that was mine will be dead. One by one.

URMILA. So your books are going to be tombs and we are going to lie there, buried alive. Waiting for death which will never come. If at all some errant reader digs us up, we'll have to live over the same predestined pages again. (*Vasudha sobs.*) Knowingly, unknowingly, you are sowing such untruths here. You think writers should do this?

RAJA. Forgive me. I really could not fathom human relationships then.

URMILA. What is your definition of 'fathoming', Rajadhakshya? Add up all previous experience, base Some calculations on that and decide—this man is this and this, his intention—this and this. Why can't you look at people without any calculations, prejudices—you know—with absolute transparency? People change by the moment. Even you are changing with each passing moment. So why can't each moment bring its own new, unclouded, clean relationship? Life will be so much simpler for you then. So much less of anguish and torment.

VASUDHA. Really! Not this horrible existence for us then. We are so unreal and yet so terribly real!

URMILA. All of the writer's prejudices bear fruit in his writing. His writing suffers much more than him. If only you had had an unclouded vision—love, compassion—

VASUDHA. Come on, Tai, let's go.

RAJA. Wait.

URMILA. Sorry, We must go. We have to.

Exit Urmila and Vausdha. Pradnya enters with drinks which nobody touches. Light on A.

PRADNYA. Why are you standing there near the books? Are you talking to them or what?

Rajadhyaksha comes back into A. C dark.

RAJA. Much as I would like to do that, do you think they would let me?

PRADNYA. Such self-indulgence!

RAJA. Now I don't have the courage to talk to them! Will I be dishonest still? I'm afraid I may be. (*Pause.*) Are you ever dishonest, young lady? To yourself? Others?

PRADNYA. Why do you ask?

RAJA. Very often I am. That's why.

PRADNYA. Perhaps we all are.

RAJA. Why are we dishonest? We live by gilding lies with truth. I've made the story of our lives—mine, Vasanti's and Uttara's—into a lie. To cover all that up, I took shelter behind a truth that was nothing but a fantasy. Or do you think there is no truth in the world? Could it be that when one does not understand the truth it turns into a lie? (*Pause.*)

PRADNYA (*gets up suddenly*). I'm going.

RAJA. Wait . . .

PRADNYA. It's late.

RAJA. Want to go home and cry? Instead, why don't you . . . (*She sobs.*) Pradnya! (*Shakes her head to say no, trying to control her sobs.*) Are you a little girl now? Come . . . (*Pradnya quietens down with a lot of effort. Pause.*)

PRADNYA. I was lying to you. (*Pause.*) We have not fought. (*Pause.*) Pramod is ready still. He thinks this is some crazy trip of mine. (*Pause.*) I told him to forget about me. We won't meet again. (*Pause.*) He's upset. He's not jealous of you. (*Pause.*)

RAJA. What is it then? (*Pause.*) What's the problem? (*Pradnya breaks down completely. Goes up to Rajadhyaksha, hugs his knees, puts her head on his knees and cries disconsolately. Gradually he realizes what it means.*) Oh God! (*He doesn't know what to do. For a moment he wants to break away. Finally he puts his hand on her head with infinite gentleness.*) Come . . . come my idiot, come . . .

Pradnya stops crying. Pulls away from him.

PRADNYA. I'll go now.

RAJA. Hm . . . Take care.

PRADNYA. Yeah.

RAJA. Let's take an off tomorrow. No dictation.

PRADNYA (*clearing her nose*). Think I'll make a scene again tomorrow? Don't worry. (*Pause.*) I didn't notice when and how I got involved. I wasn't ever going to tell you and I won't talk about it again. Never. But I won't be able to go back to Pramod.

RAJA. That's madness.

PRADNYA. I know. But that's it.

RAJA (*sad, tired*). This too, had to happen. (*Pause.*) Don't break ties, Pradnya. Bind yourself anew with each new moment. There's nothing as transient as the bonds between people. Every moment has its truth. Face it. Don't relate it to the moment that has gone. (*He goes to the window. The sky is bursting with stars.*) Come here. See this. A skyful of stars. There's nothing to bind them to us. That is the Devayani Galaxy.* It takes two million years for that light to reach Earth. The light we see now is the light from two million years ago. The galaxy may not even be there any more—who knows? We only think it is. (*Pause.*) Between man and man the distance is even greater, Pradnya. And the light each gives the other just as transient.

PRADNYA. What does one do then? How does one bridge the gap?

RAJA. You can't. Ever. That's the absolute truth.

PRADNYA. It's frightening.

RAJA. Yes, it is. Sometimes, very rarely, one gets the light of reassurance from someone else. Perhaps only for a moment. Perhaps thousands of years old. That's about enough. (*Pause.*)

PRADNYA. I'll go now.

RAJA. Come again. (*Pause.*) But I'm giving up the idea of my autobiography now.

PRADNYA. Why should I come then?

---

* Indian name for Andromeda Galaxy, 2.5 light years away from the Earth.

RAJA (*smiles*). And now even if I write, I'll have to write about you too.

PRADNYA (*smiles*). Some more vague and dishonest stuff? That will do. I'll go.

RAJA (*gently*). See you.

> *Pradnya goes out. Rajadhyaksha is disturbed. Light on B.*

VASANTI. We dug up the whole past today.

UTTARA. There IS only past. Nothing to look forward to. At times I wonder: What did we get out of all this? And what did he get, after all? But you were the worst sufferer.

VASANTI. No, Tai.

UTTARA. I may have left him. But I left him with my dignity and pride intact. The world still knows me as his wife. No one dared point a finger at me. He may not have given me anything, but I brought with me what rightfully belonged to me. You didn't get anything. He deserted you.

VASANTI. No, Tai.

UTTARA. What did he give you? (*Pause.*)

VASANTI (*looks at Uttara. It's not clear whether she's lying*). Dilip. (*Uttara is crushed.*) Dilip is his.

UTTARA (*shrieks like an animal in pain*). It's not true. (*Vasanti nods to say no.*) Want to hurt me? You still won't forgive me? I'm tired . . . exhausted . . . say it's not true.

VASANTI (*sadly*). It is, Tai.

UTTARA. You were not faithful to Devadatta?

VASANTI. Devadatta knew Dilip was Anantrao's child.

UTTARA. And he accepted it?

VASANTI. He gave me only security, Tai. There was nothing more between us.

UTTARA. It's not true.

VASANTI. Tai, it's a fact.

UTTARA. Do you mean to say that Anant used to have clandestine meetings with you?

VASANTI. He came to see Devadatta. He never talked to me. Ignored me totally. I couldn't take that. It was an offence. I wasn't going to take that insult . . . So . . . once, just once . . . I went to him . . . forget it, Tai. I wanted to see if I still had the power. I knew I had and I didn't look at him again. (*Pause.*)

UTTARA. He knows?

VASANTI. No.

UTTARA. Vasanti . . .

VASANTI. I didn't want to tell him. I didn't want to give over the reins of my life to him.

Uttara is in pieces. Staggers to the phone. Dials. At the same moment Rajadhyaksha dials from A. Both get busy signals. It happens again. Then again. And again. Both are in deep turmoil. Both finally give up and replace the receivers at the same time. Both walk back to their chairs.

UTTARA. None of us has ever seen the face of happiness. Let him see it. At least him, Vasu. (*Pause.*) Let us put our fingers in this wheel and stop it.

Vasanti keeps looking at Uttara for a long time. Then goes to the phone and dials. Phone rings in A. Rajadhyaksha does not get up. Does not move. Keeps staring at the stars. The phone keeps ringing. Lights fade out very, very gradually. Three faint spots on Rajadhyaksha, Uttara and Vasanti standing apart from one another. The walls of the house open out and slowly disappear. The sky is bursting with stars. The three of them look very small and alone under the canopy of the brilliant sky.

Curtain.